D0072635

Finance and Enterprise in Early America

DONALD R. ADAMS, Jr.

Finance and Enterprise in Early America

A Study of Stephen Girard's Bank
1812-1831

University of Pennsylvania Press
1978

Library of Congress Cataloging in Publication Data

Adams, Donald R.
  Finance and enterprise in early America.

  Includes bibliographical references and index.
  Girard Bank, Philadelphia—History.   2.   Banks and
banking—United States—History.   3.   Girard, Stephen,
1750-1831.   I.   Title.
HG2613.P54G5713   332.1′23′0974811   77-20301
ISBN 0-8122-7736-8

Printed in the United States of America.

For Sunny and Don

Contents

Tables

Acknowledgments

The task of writing this book was made easier and more enjoyable because of the cooperation and the support of a number of others.

A special thanks is due the American Council of Learned Societies, whose generous financial support made it possible to devote full time to this endeavor. As always my colleagues in the Department of Economics at Southern Illinois University at Carbondale have been helpful and encouraging.

During the research and writing stage of the manuscript, the generous cooperation of Dr. Whitfield Bell, Mr. Murphy Smith, and the staff at the Library of the American Philosophical Society in Philadelphia was invaluable. My gratitude also extends to Sister Georgine and Mrs. Susan Reilly of the John J. Wright Library at La Roche College in Pittsburgh, Pennsylvania, where the major portion of the manuscript was written. It is difficult to envision a more pleasant setting for a scholarly undertaking.

In the preparation of the manuscript my task was made easier by the diligent and skillful editing of Jane Barry and the encouragement of John McGuigan and Robert Erwin of the University of Pennsylvania Press.

Last, but by no means least, my thanks to Ms. Sue Phelan, whose skill and hard work were essential to the timely completion of the final draft.

1

Introduction

During the waning months of 1781, the military and financial fortune of the new American nation appeared to have reached a low point. Nearly six years of war had produced few victories on the battlefield and financial chaos within an unwieldy governmental apparatus. Out of these circumstances the American commercial banking system was born.

In December 1781 the Continental Congress chartered the Bank of North America in Philadelphia along lines proposed by Robert Morris. This new institution was instrumental in placing revolutionary finances on a more solid footing. The process was essentially a simple one of exchanging the bank's debt in the form of bank notes for the depreciated debt of a variety of governmental agencies. Confidence in the bank's ability to honor its liabilities was substituted for the uncertainty of the government's ability to do so. The success of this early venture stimulated imitation, and within a year of the ratification of the Treaty of Paris, the Massachusetts Bank of Boston and the Bank of New York had succeeded in obtaining charters from their respective state legislatures. During the 1790s, the number of state-chartered institutions rose from 3 to 28, with a combined authorized capital of some $17,420,000. By 1810 the number of banks had increased to 102, and in 1820 there were 341 chartered banks with a total capital of $160,980,443.[1]

To a very large degree these banks were designed to serve the commercial communities of the cities in which they were located. These commercial intermediaries substituted their liabilities in the form of bank notes or deposits for those of private individuals in the form of bills of exchange or promissory notes. The banks charged interest or exacted a discount for this service. Bank notes proved to be a welcome addition to the money supply in an era when gold and silver coins were often inadequate for carrying on the desired level of economic activity. This transformation of credit into money was viewed as nothing short of miraculous by some, and by others with understandable suspicion.

The diversity of opinion on the desirability of commercial banking is not surprising if we consider the rudimentary state of knowledge concerning banks and banking in the early nineteenth century. Few bankers realized the full potential and impact of their own institutions, let alone the consequences that flowed from changes in the banking system as a whole. Inevitably a conflict arose concerning the ultimate purposes of the banks. Should they operate to facilitate commercial transactions by specializing in the short-term credit of the local business community or provide longer-term credit and capital for development purposes?

The earliest banks tended to serve the needs of the commercial classes at the expense of the farmer or manufacturer. Such institutions issued notes secured by the obligations of merchants, which represented real transactions. If the bank was careful to lend only to those of undisputed integrity and only for short periods of time, its assets would be both sound and quite liquid. Under these circumstances the bank was assured of a steady flow of specie into its vaults as loans were repaid. With this specie it was able to meet the normal demands of its noteholders, for an essential ingredient in the acceptability of bank notes in this period was the issuing institution's willingness to convert such obligations into gold or silver on demand. Thus the bank that limited its loans and discounts to thirty- or sixty-day paper could turn its entire portfolio of earning assets into specie in one or two months by simply curtailing further lending. The capital stock of such a bank served only as collateral security for the notes issued and as a pledge for the faithful discharge of the trust reposed in the bank. The value of notes rested primarily on value received.[2] Thus the first banks exercised a function that was almost purely monetary, and their impact was almost solely on the supply of circulating medium with little or no effect on the process of long-term capital formation.[3]

Such institutions served the needs of commercial enterprises admirably but did little to satisfy the credit needs of those who required longer-term loans. The agriculturalist needed funds to buy land, to make capital improvements, or to carry him from harvest to harvest. Likewise, the manufacturer needed long-term credit until his initial investment began to yield profits. To accommodate these noncommercial borrowers, some banks departed from the "bills only" policy and extended loans for longer periods of time for noncommercial purposes. To calm the fears of stockholders and depositors, such loans were often disguised as short-term operations, with the understanding that renewals would be automatic. Many inland or "country" banks were compelled to specialize in intermediate or long-term credit by the dearth of short-term commercial paper in these areas.

Circumstances forced these early banks into what one scholar has described as a fatal hybridization of function, on the one hand issuing evidences of liability, which constituted the country's means of monetary exchange and which the banks were expected to redeem on demand, and on the other hand providing capital for fixed investments.[4] This dilemma of the commercial banking system reflected a larger division between those groups who favored a stable money supply and saw in the illiquid and unshiftable assets characteristic of long-term credit a threat to stability and those who viewed such a preoccupation with monetary stability as a barrier to capital formation. This conflict was a precursor to the "hard" money, versus "easy" money debates that punctuated later nineteenth-century monetary policy deliberation.

Because of the importance attached to early banks, they quickly assumed a quasi-public image. While bank owners and directors properly regarded their endeavors as designed to generate profits, the common man came to regard a bank as a benevolent institution, rather than a money-making one, and as possessing recognized special claims on public and legislative favor and therefore bound to accommodate the public.[5] The public was often mystified by banks, and some bankers had little desire to change this situation. Thomas Willing, president of the First Bank of the United States, wrote to the founders of the Massachusetts Bank of Boston that the world was apt to see in banking a greater mystery than there was and added, "perhaps it is right that they should do so and wonder on."[6]

Banks quickly became the focal point of broader conflicts within American society, and one's attitude toward banks and banking often betrayed more fundamental political, social, or economic beliefs. The process of granting charters often had political implications. Thus Federalist-owned banks predominated in New England, while Republican-controlled institutions were more common in the Middle Atlantic states. In 1803 President Jefferson schemed to make all banks Republican by having them share in the public deposits according to their political disposition. Moreover, those who fought against the rechartering of the First Bank of the United States viewed that struggle as a war of the middle and poorer classes of society against the rich.[7]

The dominant banking institution in the period between the Revolution and the War of 1812 was the Bank of the United States. Four-fifths of this establishment's capital stock of $10 million was held by the public, and two-fifths by the federal government. Restricted by its charter to making sixty-day loans, the BUS was authorized to "have, purchase, receive, possess, enjoy and retain . . . lands, rents, tenements, hereditaments, goods, chattels and effects . . . to an amount not exceeding the whole 15 million of dollars including the amount of the capital stock."[8] On the liability side of the ledger, the total debts of the bank, whether by bond, bill, note, or other contract, were not to exceed the amount of its capital stock.[9]

The BUS commenced operations in Philadelphia on 12 December 1791 with a twenty-year charter. Of the bank's twenty-five directors, nine were from Pennsylvania, seven from New York, four from Massachusetts, and one each from Connecticut, Maryland, North Carolina, and South Carolina. Both of its presidents, Thomas Willing (1791–1807) and David Lenox (1807–1811), were Philadelphians. Branches, referred to as offices of discount and deposit, were soon established in other major cities. Boston, New York, Baltimore, and Charleston received branches in 1792; Norfolk in 1800; Washington and Savannah in 1802; and New Orleans in 1805. Because of its size the BUS was capable of exerting some restraint on the state-chartered banks. Through its branches and the main office in Philadelphia, it continually received the bank notes of other institutions. These could be held as cash or presented to the issuing institution for redemption in specie. Because the BUS followed the latter course on a regular basis, the state banks were forced to carefully restrain their note issue in accordance with their specie reserves. As a result of this practice, the specie holdings of the BUS after 1798 amounted to about one-half of total capital, or about $5 million.[10] Unlike the modern banking system, in which an increase in the assets of the central bank encourages expansion in money supply, increases in the specie holdings of the BUS reduced the reserves of the commercial banks.

In the process of controlling the state banks, the BUS acquired more leverage as the growing number of banks and the expanded use of correspondent relationships increased the interdependence of the banking system. As the states bowed to demands for more bank charters, the established institutions slowly lost the freedom of action they had enjoyed when they possessed regional monopolies. Mathew Carey of Philadelphia observed in 1811 that "if one bank in a city reduced its discounts the others had to follow since otherwise they would have been deprived of their specie."[11] This made it possible for the BUS to exert control over all banks by controlling the operations of a few key institutions. The stability that the BUS policy brought to the financial markets was apparently appreciated by many state banks, for when its charter was about to expire, many of the nation's leading bankers earnestly worked to insure its continued operation.

Within this framework of state and federally chartered banks, various unchartered establishments continued to operate. Following the tradition of European merchant banking, these private banks carried on most of the activities of their chartered counterparts. As a rule, however, they avoided the political publicity that enveloped the latter, and since they were not subject to regulation, their affairs did not become a matter of public record.[12] These institutions were forced to exercise greater caution in lending because of the personal liability involved in their operations. On the other hand, such banks offered greater flexibility and confidentiality to their customers.

With the rapid growth of chartered banks, the importance of private houses diminished. By the time Stephen Girard's Bank began operations in 1812, the role of private banking had clearly become a supplemental one. Those that survived the competition of the chartered banks were often legislated out of existence by a variety of state "enabling acts," which limited banking functions such as note issue and discounting to duly chartered establishments. In America, as in Europe, private banks (or at least private banking) came before public banks and had long operated with little or no regulation. The times now demanded public regulation of banks and greater specialization in the area of finance. Thus in America, banking provides the first clear-cut example of the replacement of private ownership by the corporate form throughout an entire range of economic activity.

Private banking did not disappear, of course. Indeed, the number and size of such private institutions increased as the financial needs of the business community became more complex and sophisticated. However, private bankers were increasingly barred from activities commonly associated with commercial banking, the most lucrative of which, from the point of view of the banker, was the ability to issue bank notes. Girard's bank, however, was able to continue many of these functions, a fact which set it apart from other private institutions of the day. Indeed, its survival and success were to a large degree based on this uniqueness.

In America, where private banking was often closely associated with large merchandising operations, Girard was again the exception.[13] Although he carried on a substantial mercantile business, Girard kept his banking operations scrupulously separated from his other commercial pursuits. He boasted to Alexander Baring in 1815 that "my commercial Capital enables me to sell my goods on credit and to carry on my maritime business throughout Cash in hand without the aid of Discounts."[14] Unlike other private bankers, Girard did not shun publicity or controversy and was often at the center of the era's most important financial developments. Through sheer size and tenacity, he was able to survive the opposition of the chartered banks of Philadelphia and thwart the application of state laws to his operations. For a short while at least, the Bank of Stephen Girard stood almost alone among the growing number of corporate banks as a force to be reckoned with and a classic example of individual enterprise. To some, his bank represented the last remnant of an outdated, commercially oriented, and mercantilist past. To others, his bank served as an important link between the eighteenth-century preoccupation with trade and commerce and the nineteenth-century passion for domestic growth and development, between the era of private bankers and the era of corporate banking.

To view Girard as primarily a banker would, of course, be misleading. His success in other commercial areas was already legendary by the time his banking house commenced operations. Generally recognized as one of he nation's richest men, his private fleet of ships (the "philosopher" vessels—*Rousseau, Voltaire, Helvetius,* and *Montesquieu*) carried Girard's commercial pennant to the far reaches of the world. As simultaneously one of the most important merchants in the trade between the United States and northern Europe and in America's far eastern trade, Girard was part of an intricate international network of commercial intelligence and finance. He was the wealthiest merchant in Philadelphia and, with the possible exception of his friend John Jacob Astor, in the entire nation.

Despite all his mercantile concerns, Girard found time to perpetuate the traditional link to the soil so strong among the French. He spent part of nearly every day on his large farm in Passyunk near the juncture of the Schuylkill and Delaware rivers. Here he experimented with new varieties of trees, practiced experimental agricultural techniques, and presumably banished for a while the pressures of the business world.

In short, Girard was a consumate businessman in an era when commercially successful individuals dominated American society. While our story deals primarily with early nineteenth-century banking, we should not forget that Stephen Girard's Bank, much more than most, reflected the energy, zeal, and commercial and economic philosophy of its founder and principal director.

2

The Birth of a
Banking Enterprise

Stephen Girard's Bank was, to a very large extent, the direct result of three major historical events: the continuation of the Continental wars following the fragile and short-lived Peace of Amiens; the disruption of international trade during the Embargo and Nonintercourse periods; and the failure of the First Bank of the United States to obtain a new charter in 1811. There were other courses open to Girard for the application of his sizable fortune, and the chain of events that led to his decision to become a private banker is an interesting one.

Stephen Girard became an American almost by accident.[1] Born in Bordeaux in 1750, the young Frenchman was master of a small vessel engaged in trade between New York and the West Indies when he was forced into the port of Philadelphia by rough weather and the British fleet. The year was 1776, and the American struggle for independence had just begun. The war and the British occupation of Philadelphia induced Girard to open a small store in Mount Holly, New Jersey. With the departure of the British from Philadelphia, Girard returned to Philadelphia, became a citizen of Pennsylvania, and opened a new business in North Water Street on the Delaware. Girard's foreign operations concentrated at first on the West Indian trade but later expanded to Europe and Asia. Skill, persistance, and careful planning insured Girard's success, and by the first decade of the nineteenth century he was a man of considerable wealth and international reputation.[2]

With the coming of the Napoleonic Wars, American foreign trade prospered. As a nonbelligerent, the United States engaged in the carrying trade between the warring nations with virtual immunity from the severe sanctions mutually imposed by Napoleon and the British Parliament. As the Continental wars intensified, however, the risks associated with maritime trade grew rapidly. America found it increasingly difficult to maintain her treasured and lucrative neutrality, and Girard perceived sooner than most that an era was quickly coming to an end. He now pondered the correct course to pursue in light of his situation. He had ships, cargoes, and funds spread all over the European continent, and a large share of his fortune lay, not in Philadelphia, but in Amsterdam, Hamburg, Saint Petersburg, Copenhagen, Riga, London, and other trading centers. By the year 1807 Girard had decided to act.

In a letter to his London correspondents, Baring Brothers, on 31 October 1807, Girard recounted the "gloomy" situation that now existed between the European belligerents and the United States and indicated that "those unforeseen circumstances called on my immediate attention to send a confidential agent to your continent in view to represent my interest in the same manner as if I was there myself. . . ."[3] For this purpose, Girard dispatched Mahlon Hutchinson, Jr., a long-time apprentice in his own countinghouse. Girard evidently did not anticipate the need to repatriate all of his funds from Europe at that time, for he informed Baring Brothers that "having some funds on your Continent I do not presume that Mr. Hutchinson will have occasion to draw large sums from your house unless circumstances should render it necessary. . . ."[4]

But circumstances were changing rapidly, and President Jefferson was under great pressure to act decisively. To forestall further friction with both France and England, Jefferson imposed an embargo on all foreign trade on 22 December 1807. Girard's response was immediate. Writing to Baring Brothers on the day after Christmas, he observed that news of the embargo had no doubt reached London and indicated that he had instructed Hutchinson "to invest all the funds . . . in Europe in certain species of property. . . ."[5]

By January 1808, Girard saw an opportunity to transfer his sterling credits with Baring Brothers to dollars at a profit. Consequently, on 4 January 1808 he informed his London agents that "should exchange on England continue at the present rate of 75 percent I will prevail myself on you for the greatest part of the funds which I have in your hands."[6] By February, exchange on London stood at 175–177.10 currency to £100 sterling, or $4.66 to 4.73. In April Girard indicated that he had refused to negotiate exchange at 177½, "expecting that in a few days 80 percent will be easily obtained."[7] In fact, that same day, Girard was able to draw sixty-day payable notes on Baring Brothers for £4897.9.10 and added, "I have effected that negotiation at 80 percent, should exchange keep up I will extend my drawings to nearly the amount of my funds in your hands."[8] Exchange rates continued to improve, standing at 182½ on 12 April 1808 and 185 currency to 100 sterling on 3 May. On the latter date, Girard noted that he had negotiated about one-fourth of his account with Baring Brothers at that rate and indicated his intention to transfer some Amsterdam funds to London to expand these exchange operations.[9] Throughout June, Girard managed to negotiate some £12,000 sterling in bills on London at 185 and ordered a wholesale transfer of funds from Amsterdam to London. "Should you have sufficient reason to believe that this country will escape the present prospect of being involved in the European War," said Girard, "and that American funds in England will be perfectly safe please to request Messrs. Hope & Co. to remit on my Account and on the most advantageous terms to Messrs. Baring Brothers & Co. of London as far as forty thousand pounds Sterling. . . ."[10] If the exchange rate between the guilder and the pound was such that a profit of 3 percent or more was possible on the transaction, then Hutchinson was authorized to increase the transfer to £60,000. The same letter provides a clue as to why Girard was concentrating his funds in London. Quite apart from the more favorable rate of exchange, "Bills on London may at all times be negotiated with more facility and to a greater amount than those drawn on France or Holland."[11]

By July 1808 Girard was exploring alternative means of remitting his assets to the United States. He instructed Baring Brothers to purchase American stocks and "to invest on my account in 3 and 6 percent as far as ten thousand pounds Sterling provided the price of the former does not exceed fifty-four or fifty-five and the latter ninety percent."[12] Exchange on London did not continue to improve, and by October it was on the decline. Girard attributed the deterioration in terms to "a large amount of British Government Bills which are from time to time brought for sale to this City."[13]

Domestic and international politics now began to play a more prominent role in Girard's decisions. With Jefferson under pressure to repeal the Embargo Act and New England flirting with nullification, Girard observed that "our political affairs have a gloomy prospect," and instructed Baring Brothers "to suspend the purchase of stock on my account until further notice."[14] In January 1809 a Force Act was passed by the Congress. Under its provisions federal officials could seize, without warrants, goods which it was suspected were bound for foreign ports. Girard's response to this legislation showed a trace of desperation. "Since writing you on the 3rd Ult.," he told Baring Brothers, "new circumstances have rendered probable that shortly there will be a change in our commercial situation. Fearful of its results I beg that you will as soon as possible invest my funds in your hands in Public Stock of the U. States. I give you no limits," he added, "please to act as if it was for yourselves and to keep said stock in your hands subject to my order."[15] Girard apparently realized that should trade between the United States and England be suspended, all merchants with funds in London or other British cities would seek alternatives to merchandise for the repatriation of these assets. Both Bank of the United States stock and U. S. government stock suited this purpose well, and Girard wished to convert some of his balances to this form before the sterling price of such financial assets was bid up. Granting such license over his own property was out of character for Girard and is an indication of the gravity with which he viewed the situation. The situation was quickly remedied the following week when the Barings were instructed to buy 6 percent stock only if it could be purchased at an 8 percent discount and even then only to a limit of £10,000.[16]

Jefferson reluctantly signed a bill repealing the embargo on 1 March 1809, and Girard immediately seized the opportunity to utilize some of his European funds. Hutchinson was ordered to draw on Amsterdam and London, if necessary, to provide "hard money" for the ship *Voltaire*'s intended Canton voyage and for the *Montesquieu*'s venture to "Bengal or China."[17]

These were particularly difficult times for Girard as each new rumor of impending conflict or political action on the part of the American, British, or French governments profoundly affected his decisions. The frequent reversals in his financial decisions simply underscored the mounting uncertainty surrounding future political and commercial relations between Europe and America. As 1809 wore on, Girard became increasingly concerned about the safety of his funds in Europe. "Keep in view," he wrote Hutchinson, "that I wish you to place my funds into safe hands subject to my order and I repeat you that I prefer to receive no Interest, than to run any risk whatever."[18] As relations between the United States and Britain became increasingly strained, Alexander Baring himself addressed Girard on the subject. In reply Girard gravely noted that "Your observations on the subject of the imminent risk which our maritime commerce is attended with has received my serious attention and will have its influence on my future operations."[19] Moreover, Girard expressed regret "that the British Government has not sanctioned the arrangements made by Mr. Erskine," and added, "How far their nonadherence will prove fatal to the Commerce of both Countries, time alone will ascertain. . . ."[20]

The senior Baring's letter obviously had a sobering effect on Girard, for the following day he instructed Hutchinson to devote serious attention to the accumulation of funds in London. "Although I have the greatest confidence in the responsibility of the London house who is charged with my affairs," he wrote, "yet a uncertainty of an unfavorable change may call for a removal of my Funds in their hands, either in investing them in United States Bank Stock or in Public Stocks if obtainable, otherwise to invest one-half of said Funds, in Goods of a quick sale suitable for this market, which you will ship to my address per first vessel for this Port and to lodge the other half in a safe house on the Continent of Europe subject to my orders."[21]

Despite his efforts, Girard's account in London grew over the year and by the end of 1809 stood at £102,642.6.1. Transfers from Hope and Company in Amsterdam to London alone accounted for £131,003.5.9.[22] The year 1810 saw no substantial improvement in relations between the United States and Britain, and the dilemma that faced Girard was rapidly taking form. He ordered Baring Brothers in May 1810 to stop purchases of American stock until further notice, "unless it can be obtained at par calculating the Exchange between your place and this at that rate. . . ."[23] He informed the Barings that in Philadelphia, "Stock or Shares of the U. States Bank are selling at present from eight to ten percent above par," but noted that "should Congress refuse to renew the Charter of that Institution its stockholders will experience a great loss. Public stock offers at present the greatest advantage unless we should be involved in a war. Three percents are now selling at 65 percent."

Girard was vulnerable from several different directions. Macon's Bill Number 2 provided for an interlude in the commercial warfare between the United States and Europe, but continued intercourse was dependent on concessions from either France or Britain. Thus at any time, trade with England or the Continent could be closed down, making the purchase of British goods for import a risky undertaking.[24]

The alternatives to shipping goods to the United States were purely financial transfers. Here two possibilities presented themselves. United States government stocks could be purchased. However, the fluctuating exchange rate and the threat of war made this an equally precarious undertaking. Should war break out, the American government would be forced to borrow, flooding the market with new stock and driving down the price.[25] The other option was buying shares in the Bank of the United States. Of course, there was a distinct possibility that the bank's charter would not be renewed. Stockholders of the bank and others had memorialized Congress for a renewal of the charter in 1808 and again in 1810.[26] In both instances Congress debated renewal but took no action. Bank shares were selling well above par in 1810, and many feared that the failure to obtain a new charter would destroy the market for bank stock, as the institution would be forced to liquidate its assets. The market for BUS stock in London was particularly active, since nearly 70 percent of the stock was concentrated in British hands. Girard's first reaction to this problem was to attempt to spread the risk among the alternatives by shipping goods to the United States, buying government stock, and purchasing bank shares. He postponed the decision on how to employ these substantial assets once repatriated.

Girard began the year 1810 wth a balance of £102,642.6.1 to his account at Baring Brothers. During the year he managed to transfer £45,440.15.7 to the United States, but £59,500.1.11 in remittances from the Continent to London increased his balance there to £116,701.-12.5 by the beginning of 1811.[27] On 23 February 1811, Girard instructed Baring Brothers to advise his Hamburg agents, Schwartz Brothers and Company, of the best way to make an "end of my concerns under their care."[28] Indicating his aversion to risky maritime ventures, Girard noted that "all the ships which I had in the North Ports of the Continent of Europe have returned to this, one with German goods and three with Russia [*sic*] Cargoes." He added that in Philadelphia, "business are [*sic*] of present extremely dull and money very scarce. . . ." The latter he attributed, in part, to the approaching dissolution of the United States Bank, "which renders the officers of that Institution very cautious."[29]

On 22 May 1811, Girard begged Baring Brothers to "continue purchasing some kind of stock on my account as far as Fifty Thousand pounds Sterling. I do not limit the price, my object is simlpy to realize in this country a part of my property."[30] By June Girard increased the tempo of his withdrawal from the Continent, ordering his agents in Riga, Stralsund, Copenhagen, Hamburg, and Holstein to close the sale of his goods there and remit the proceeds to Baring Brothers "as fast as practicable."[31] In a letter of 5 June 1811 to Baring Brothers, Girard gave what may be the first indication of his interest in private banking activities. Having decided to curtail his maritime operations, he expressed his desire "to retain here the remainder of my funds which I will keep in activity by discounting notes."[32]

As early as the spring of 1810, Girard had authorized David Parish to act on his behalf and assist Hutchinson in clearing up his European accounts.[33] Now Girard dispatched two more agents—Charles N. Bancker, a young Philadelphia merchant, and Joseph Curwen of the same city. Bancker's primary mission was to buy merchandise for the ship *Good Friends,* and he was authorized to utilize up to £50,000 Sterling for that purpose. Bancker left New York for London in August 1811. Curwen, who was to concentrate on settling financial matters, sailed for the same city aboard the *Good Friends,* which left Philadelphia about 1 August.[34]

The Bank of the United States, thwarted in its petition for a federal charter, turned to the Pennsylvania legislature during its fall session of 1811. The prospect of success in the state legislature renewed interest in the bank's stock, and on 23 December, Girard expressed his sincere hope to Curwen in London that he had "invested all unappropriated funds in United States Bank shares even at £95 Sterling per share."[35] He added that "the Trustees of the United States Bank have applied for a charter to our legislature now sitting and it is confidentially expected that they will obtain their goal." Girard was still optimistic about the charter of the BUS in Pennsylvania in early January 1812. He noted in a letter to Curwen that "the rate which you quote American Stock offers a real loss. United States Bank shares present a more favorable prospect particularly if the Charter is obtained. That kind of stock now sells at 98 percent and if the Bank is permitted to go into operation the shares will instantly rise to upwards of 10 percent above par."[36] In a final thought, Girard predicted that "the application made by the Trustees of the late U.S. Bank to the Legislature of this State will meet great opposition nevertheless I am still of opinion that there is two chances to one in favor of a charter being granted to them."

Given the difficulties involved, Girard and his agents in Europe had been reasonably successful in bringing a major portion of his holdings safely back to Philadelphia. Girard's account at Baring Brothers was £116,701.12.5 at the outset of 1811, to which he added an inflow of Continental remittances of some £77,894.1.4 during the course of the year. Nonetheless, his balance on 8 January 1812 amounted to £40,639.4.2.[37] Thus, during the year, £153,856.9.7 was returned to the United States in one fashion or another. According to Girard, the remittances consisted of £86,912.10.6 in American 6 percent stock at 12 percent above par and United States Bank shares at about £94.10 per share, plus a cargo of British manufactures worth £66,943.19.1.[38]

The fate of the Bank of the United States, at least in Pennsylvania, was decided in January. Girard informed Baring Brothers on 23 January that "On the 20th Instant . . . a large majority . . . have voted against a Charter to the Institution," and requested that this information be forwarded to Curwen, since it was essential to his Continental interest "that it should reach its address at an early period."[39] The same day Girard wrote to Curwen informing him of the legislature's decision, even though "the bonus offered was ten percent on the Capital and if required to Loan at any time $500,000 to the State of Pennsylvania at the rate of 5 percent per annum."[40] It was probable, added Girard, that "the United States will be under the necessity to open a New Loan which of course will depreciate the present stock."

The Bank of the United States now applied to the state of New York for a charter, but the outlook there was dim. Girard lamented to Curwen that "it is pretty well understood that the late Bank of the United States will fail in obtaining a charter. Their last resource was in New York where the Governor . . . recommends to the Legislature not to grant a Charter to any new Bank."[41] However, reported Girard, "I had several conversations with some of the Trustees of that Bank particularly with the President and Cashier. If my information is correct there is no doubt that . . . their Capital will not divide less than four hundred dollars per share.

"Should you judge advantageous to invest the remainder of my funds that way I leave with you to act for best of my Interests."

By concentrating on the purchase of BUS shares, Girard had made the best of a difficult situation. Had the BUS obtained a charter to operate in Pennsylvania, its shares would have immediately increased in value—by Girard's estimate to some 10 percent above par, or $440— and could have been profitably disposed of or retained as a dividend-paying investment. Should the charter fail, Girard now knew that the shares would divide for no less than $400. The failure of the BUS and the probability of war would force the government to seek a loan from the public, which would drive down the price of the 3 and 6 percent stock that constituted the principal investment alternative to the BUS shares.[42] Having successfully returned over one million dollars worth of assets from Europe to the United States, the question now arose of how best to employ such funds in the face of a disrupted foreign trade, an impending war, and an unsettled capital market.[43]

The decision to operate a private banking house was only one option open to Girard in early 1812. He could have been content to devote full time to his massive mercantile and real estate interests in Philadelphia.[44] As the largest stockholder in the BUS, he would have participated profitably in its liquidation.[45] Still another option would have been to invest in the proposed $6 million Bank of New York. Actually, this proposed institution was to be the successor to the New York branch of the BUS, which was eventually chartered as the Bank of America. Of its $6 million capital, $5 million was to consist of BUS shares. Each subscriber would receive four shares of the new bank stock in return for one of the old. In fact, Girard followed closely the attempt of the Bank of America to obtain a New York charter. However, hopes for its success diminished significantly in March 1812. On 1 April 1812, David Parish informed Girard from New York that on "Friday last at the moment of taking the final question on the American Bank Bill in the Senate of the State of New York, and which would have been passed beyond all doubt the Governor prorogued the Legislature until the 21st of May in order to defeat the passage of that bill.[46]

Girard's private banking venture was all the more precarious since a great deal of opposition to such an enterprise could be anticipated. The established Philadelphia banks were apt to view the formation of a large, uncharterd institution directed by an aggressive and powerful owner as a direct threat to their own pre-eminent position and to react accordingly. On the other hand, those who opposed the BUS were likely to view Girard's bank as a continuation of its hated predecessor. Girard's purchase of the BUS property on Third Street and his retention of George Simpson as his cashier did little to dispel such suspicions. Thus for wholly different reasons, "Girard was opposed by both conservative and radical financial interests of the state."[47]

The opening of a private banking house, however, allowed Girard to capitalize the value of his BUS shares at par, continue to collect dividends on the same, and profit from the discount and interest resulting from the earning assets of his bank. The same was true to a lesser extent with respect to his holdings of government stock. Moreover, the capitalization of BUS and government stocks into a banking enterprise reduced the probability of a large, forced liquidation. The latter was all the more certain if the bank was run on a very conservative basis.

Regardless of when the final decision to operate a bank was made, we know that by the first week in May arrangments for the opening of Stephen Girard's Bank were all but complete. Uncharacteristically, Girard was out of the city during the better part of early May, but kept in touch with events through J. H. Roberjot, one of his Philadelphia agents.[48] Such an event was not to be kept secret for long, and soon Philadelphia was astir with rumors of the impending reopening of the BUS. Girard's absence conveniently removed him from the scene and the necessity of answering a barrage of queries. Indeed, he seemed to enjoy from afar the excitement that his activities were engendering. "I observe with pleasure," he wrote to Roberjot, "that our citizens are recreating themselves in planning for me the best mode of disposing of the late U.S. Bank, but I am sorry to notice that they are going so far as to insult some respectable and ancient officers of that institution, by saying that I have purchased them."[49] Roberjot too seemed to handle the speculation with a light touch. He informed Girard on 8 May that "several others called to make enquiry, if you were going to establish a

Bank. To get rid of them I tell them you reserve the House for an Hospital. . . . ."⁵⁰

Most inquiries were of a casual nature like that of M. Payan, whose letter of 5 May indicated, "I hear by public report that having purchased the bank buildings formerly of the U.S. your intention is to establish at once the kind of business for which it was intended, a project well worthy of your name."⁵¹ Other communications were of a more serious nature, such as the two from Jared Ingersoll, a prominent Philadelphia lawyer and one of Girard's legal advisors. "There is a report in circulation," wrote Ingersoll, "that you and some others are about to purchase the house late belonging to the Bank of the U.S. for purpose of Banking.

"Pray let me see you before you conclude the bargain. I wish to give you a caution upon the subject in relation to the late law or act of Assembly."⁵² Again, on 5 May, Ingersoll warned that "if the report be true that you are about to purchase the House belonging to the late Bank of the United States, I think it would be best to have it conveyed to some other person so as to avoid any claim of Dower."⁵³ Thus only days before his bank commenced operations, one of Girard's most trusted legal advisors knew of his momentous venture only through common gossip and public rumors. Unlikely as it may seem, it appears that Girard made the most important financial decision of his career, and one fraught with potential legal problems, without the benefit of counsel.

The first two weeks of May also brought a large number of letters from individuals seeking employment at Girard's new banking house. By far the most interesting of these inquiries was that of Erick Bollman, the well-known writer on economics and advocate of the commercial banking system. In his letter of 5 May, Bollman lamented that "my lettering Pursuits yield me some Reputation but no pecuniary Emolument of any Consequences." However, he continued, "if the business, in which you contemplate to engage, afforded a Situation, yielding an income of perhaps Twelve or Fifteen hundred dollars a year, it would procure me ease of mind and be at the same time not incompatible with the pursuit of lettering Objects. . . . I should consider the situation the more satisfactory as it would bring me more and more in contact with a Gentleman of your Intelligence and Liberality."⁵⁴ Evidently he received no answer to his plea, for he again addressed Girard on 20 May, this time in French. He enclosed pamphlets dealing with money and banking, and noted that "if you find the work satisfactory, if you believe that it will be of use to the public, and also to myself to continue my researches on similar subjects—kindly place me a little at ease by rendering me the small service of which I spoke to you. As the head of the bank it would cost you very little." Bollman added, "I have on hand an important work 'Elements of Political Economy.' One must be at ease to do this work well. In Europe men-of-letters often have their patrons. Be mine. I will show my gratitude publicly in a way which, perhaps, will please you."[55]

Bollman was not hired but a staff was necessary, and Girard authorized the employment of seven individuals as well as George Simpson, the cashier. He stipulated that salaries, which were to commence on 18 May, were to be the same as those paid by the defunct Bank of the United States. Hired were:

Joseph Roberts, teller at $1650 per annum
Mathias Gebler, receiving teller at $1430 per annum
John Heaton, first bookkeeper at $1320 per annum
William Fawcett, second bookkeeper at $990 per annum
Nathaniel Lewis, discount clerk at $990 per annum
William Forrest, runner at $880 per annum
Samuel Carter, porter at $495 per annum[56]

As the date of the opening of the bank drew near, Girard at last became concerned about the legality of his venture and sought an opinion from Jared Ingersoll and Alexander J. Dallas. Their brief is dated 20 May 1812 and was sent to Girard a full two days following the commencement of operations. The lawyers were required to distinguish between Girard's new bank and those institutions forbidden by the 1810 prohibition of unincorporated banks under Pennsylvania law.[57] Their opinion is interesting and can be divided into three basic sections: first, a description of Girard's proposed operations; second, a discussion of their legality; and third, a consideration of the functions such a bank might legally perform. It states that "Stephen Girard proposes Singly upon his own capital to establish a Bank in the city of Philadelphia, for discounting promissory notes and Bills of Exchange. The business of his establishment will be managed in a manner similar to the management of the Incorporated banks, and at a considerable expense and trouble, not common to the employment of money in private loans upon interest." The attempt here was apparently to distinguish Girard's contemplated activities from those of private merchants making private loans by citing the scale of operations and administrative costs involved.

The attorneys then carefully approached the question of the bank's legal status. "By an act of Assembly passed on the 28th of March, 1808, it was declared, that every member of a voluntary association for the purposes of Banking should be individually liable, for the debts of the Association, any agreement with the creditors to the contrary notwithstanding." However, they continued, "the act of 19th March, 1810 declared it to be unlawful for any unincorporated association of persons, to do any act which an incorporated Banking Company might lawfully do; for any person to be a customer of such unincorporated Bank; and for any person to circulate its notes. Any individual citizen of Pennsylvania may still however, engage in the Business of Banking as he may in any other lawful pursuit." Girard's bank was not incorporated, but neither was it an unincorporated association. It was an institution owned and operated by an individual citizen and therefore legal under the terms of the law of 28 March 1810.[58]

The lawyers now addressed the question of what activities were allowed to such a private bank. "The Business of Banking," they asserted, "does not consist entirely in buying notes or bills of exchange; but also in *discounting* them; or in other words, it consists in lending money upon the joint security of the parties to notes, or bills of exchange." Pennsylvania law stated that "no person shall, directly or indirectly, for any bonds or contracts take for the loan or use of money, or any other commodities above the value of £6, for the forebearance of £100, or the value thereof, for one year, and so proportionally for any greater or less sum." Ingersoll and Dallas noted that if a banker retains £6 at the time of a loan, he is charging £6 for the use of £94, not £100.[59] "This practice," contended the attorneys, "is followed in every incorporated Bank in Pennsylvania, by the late Bank of the United States and by the Bank of England as well as other British banks." Thus, they concluded," there is no difference in legal rights of an individual and of a corporation employed in the Business of Banking, except where the charter of incorporation expressly introduces a distinction. . . ." Therefore, "we are of opinion, that Mr. Girard is entitled to discount Promissory notes and Bills of Exchange, in the same manner as the Incorporated Banks, by deducting the interest at the time of discount."[60]

Fortified by the legal advice of his lawyers, Girard officially informed the state of his *fait accompli*. In a letter addressed to Governor Simon Snyder, dated 23 May 1812, Girard stated that "the unfavorable prospect of our Maritime Commerce has induced me to appropriate some of my funds to discount negotiable notes, for that purpose I have purchased from the Trustees of the late Bank of the United States, their Banking House and appurtanances [*sic*] situated in this City, South Third Street and there intend to transact on my private account the Banking business as far as prudence will permit."[61]

The agreement to purchase the premises of the late BUS was reached on 9 May 1812, and a memorandum of the agreement provides details of the transfer.[62] Girard was to receive in fee simple the banking house, the grounds, and the house and lot occupied by George Simpson, "to-gether with all and singular their respective appurtanaces [*sic*] and the Iron Chests, Scales, Furniture and apparatus now in use in said Bank. . . ." The price was set at $115,000, "payable in six months from the 1st day of June, 1812."[63] Girard had the option of delaying payment until 1 May 1813 by paying interest from the first day of December 1812. The trustees were to receive the use of certain facilities necessary for the process of closing out BUS affairs. An indenture of David Lenox and others with Stephen Girard specified that the trustees were to have the use of the director's room, the president's room with the vault adjoining it, the north side of the banking room, and one large vault below, as well as desks, cases, and other furniture and equipment essential to the liquidation of the bank's business. For these premises the trustees were to pay annually one peppercorn rent, should it be demanded.[64]

A final legal matter remained: as Girard was the sole proprietor of the bank, what would happen in the event of his death? Girard and his attorneys worked out a trust arrangement with a group of well-known Philadelphia citizens. The trustees were David Lenox, former board member and trustee of the BUS; Robert Waln, merchant and board member of the Bank of North America and the Philadelphia Insurance Company; Joseph Ball, board member of the Union Insurance Company; and George Simpson, cashier. This group was to insure that if Girard died, "no delay or obstruction in the usual payment of the *monies deposited* with him may ensue; but that all business may be transacted with the like promptitude and punctuality, as it could during the lifetime of Mr. Girard." This "places his business," stated the trust agreement, "on the same secure foundation, in regard to the public, as that of the incorporated Banks."[65] Since the arrangement more or less implied a liquidation process, it was not identical to that associated with corporate institutions.

Having clarified, to his own satisfaction, the legal status of his venture, Girard now proceeded to gather the financial resources that would form the foundation of his bank. Girard's plan was to carefully and method-ically build up the capital stock of his bank over the first years of its existence. The first entry, designated "cash," consisted of three checks drawn by Girard on local banks—the first, on the Bank of Pennsylvania, for $56,000.00; the second, on the Bank of the United States for $13,414.31; and the third on the Bank of North America for $2,000.00.[66] The total of $71,414.31 was credited to the capital stock of Stephen Girard's Bank on 18 May 1812.[67] On 1 June, an additional $556,125.89 was credited to capital stock. It consisted of:

City Corporation loan	$ 43,200.00
3% stock of U.S.	68,152.32
6% stock of U.S.	61,671.37
6% Louisiana stock	3,902.20
948 shares of BUS	379,200.00
	$556,125.89

The United States stocks were listed at "first cost," and the BUS shares at par. The 3 percent stock was purchased between 29 May 1810 and 11 December 1811 and was valued nominally at $104,089.07. The 6 percent stock was purchased between 17 May 1811 and 1 January 1812 and had a nominal value of $107,455.68. The Louisiana stock was purchased on the 17 December 1811 at a price of 111½ per share.

On 15 June Girard added to capital stock most of the proceeds from the sale of the cargo of the *Good Friends*. This entry was titled "bills and notes received for sundry notes deposited for collection" and amounted to $450,842.38. A personal check on his own account at Stephen Girard's Bank for $125,298.80 on 30 June, a 2 July deposit of $2,200.00 in Philadelphia City Corporation stock, plus another personal check for $100,000.00 on 30 November brought the year-end capital stock to $1,305,881.38. An entry to cash (Bank and house) on 1 December 1812 indicates that Girard paid for the BUS premises out of capital account, and then credited a new asset entry—Bank Estate—by the amount of $115,000.00. In this fashion he was able to carry the bank estate as part of capital stock.

Girard continued to add to capital stock throughout 1813. On 4 January 1813, $22,544.40 in discount and interest was added, and on 22 May $73,000.00 in 6 percent stock, plus $67,850.53 in discount and interest, which had accumulated between 1 July and 31 December. A $40,186.51 addition of "sundries" and a subtraction of $9,462.82 for his personal account produced a capital stock of $1.5 million on 1 January 1814. Additions came less frequently after 1813, and capital stock reached its ultimate level of $3 million in January 1827.

Girard's first priority was clearly to establish his institution on a par with the other major banks of the city. To do this he was willing to forgo profits and the accumulation of surplus. The bank's profit and loss accounts show no net balance for 1812, indicating that nearly all net income (mostly in the form of discount or interest on the public debt) was channeled into capital stock. Not until mid-1814 did the profit and loss figures indicate a respectable balance of $13,748.53.[68] Interest income for 1812 was credited to capital stock, as was the $38,900.19 in interest income for 1813.[69] Not until July 1814 was a sizable sum of interest income ($22,099.26) credited to profit and loss. The first surplus account of Stephen Girard's Bank does not appear until 2 January 1816.[70]

It was precisely this ability to reject present income in favor of greater size and financial power that made Girard a feared competitor of the other city banks. The latter had stockholders accustomed to receiving substantial annual dividends, and the responsibility of generating profits on a regular basis clearly limited their flexibility. Add to this flexibility the residual prestige of the Bank of the United States in some circles and Girard's enormous personal fortune, and it is little wonder that Girard's bank was not warmly received into the Chestnut Street financial community.

Soon after Girard began operations, the trustees of the late Bank of the United States decided to provide for a special arrangement betwen themselves and his bank. Girard was to be designated to receive and disburse payments for the trustees, and they, in turn, were to maintain their account with his banking house. This account was substantial, amounting to $815,289.63 on 1 October 1812.[71] However, establishing this arrangement on a permanent basis was not without its difficulties, as the records show. On 5 November 1813, Girard received a memorandum of agreement between himself and David Lenox for the trustees of the BUS. This agreement specified that Girard was to pay 3 percent interest on all funds deposited by the trustees. The interest thus paid was to be calculated monthly on the balance at the end of the month. On its part, Stephen Girard's Bank might terminate the agreement at any time by paying to the trustees at such time 3 percent interest on their deposits at the beginning of that month. The trustees, in turn, might withdraw their funds at any time, but Girard was not obligated to pay interest for that part of the month that had run out. According to the Lenox memorandum, the agreement was to become effective immediately, and a month's interest was to be considered due on 30 November 1813.[72] Moreover, Lenox had scheduled a meeting of a trustees' committee for noon on 5 November at Girard's bank to settle the matter.

Girard's reply to Lenox was immediate and animated. "As the object of the Contract alluded to, is to charge me an Interest on the unemployed funds resulting from those which said Trustees from time to time confided in my Bank for the purpose of paying the Dividends due to the Stockholders and other Creditors of the late Bank of the United States, I will for the present limit my remarks to the conversation I had with you on 2nd November at my bank in which I explained my intentions and put these in writing immediately thereafter. Should you wish to refresh your memory, the contents of said writing will at any time be communicated to you by Mr. George Simpson."[73]

The agreement referred to by Girard stated that interest was to be

3 percent on sums over $100,000 (that is, interest paid on multiples of
$100,000, $200,000, $300,000, etc.) and was to commence on 1
January 1814. Girard's record stated that interest was to be calculated
and paid every three months and was to be credited to an interest
account of the BUS. Finally, all funds resulting from the liquidation of
the BUS were to be deposited in Stephen Girard's Bank for the purpose
of paying dividends, debts, and expenses of the BUS.[74] Referring to the
agreement of 2 November, Girard assured Lenox that "if my proposal
does not meet the approbation of the Trustees of the late Bank of the
United States, that the very identical gold which they have confided in
my Bank . . . is at their disposal and if required will be returned to
them at the same rate as it was received."[75] While it is difficult to see
how Lenox and Girard could have formed such different recollections
of a conversation only three days old, no permanent damage appears to
have resulted to the relationship between the trustees and Stephen
Girard's Bank. The former maintained an account with Girard until the
dissolution of the bank in 1831.[76]

Even before the dispute over the terms of the agreement, Girard was
inconvenienced by his relationship with the trustees. On 9 March 1813,
for example, Simpson was forced to write to D. A. Smith, cashier of the
Mechanic's Bank of Baltimore, that "it is not convenient at present to
discount the notes mentioned as the Trustees of the late Bank of the
United States have declared a dividend of seven percent payable on first
of April next which is much more than was expected and will occasion
a considerable demand in Mr. Girard's Bank."[77] On this occasion and
again on 18 March, Simpson was forced to request remittances from
Smith and the Farmer's Bank of Lancaster to meet the demands of the
BUS dividend.[78] Thus while the deposits of the trustees of the late BUS
were a public indication of confidence in Girard's new bank, they were
also subject to rapid withdrawal, forcing the restriction of more profitable banking activities and making Girard's "special arrangement" with
the trustees at best a mixed blessing.

At about the same time as Girard's bank commenced operations in
Philadelphia, Joseph Curwen in London was desperately attempting to
settle the banker's affairs in the face of imminent hostilities. On 16 May
1812, Curwen reported that Girard's funds appeared as safe as could be
expected under the circumstances and included details on the sum owed
in other cities on the Continent.[79] Increasingly alarmed at the prospect
of war, Curwen sent a final dispatch on 10 June. "The great difference,"
he noted, "in the price of all kinds of American Stocks, between the
United States and this country makes any investment of that kind out of
the question. The low rate of exchange will I take it for granted prevent

you negotiating your bills as long as you think your money safe—As I see no immediate prospect of an immediate change for the better and being perfectly satisfied about the safety of the property even in case of a war, I have determined on returning home and on leaving your funds in this country."[80]

Girard penned a letter to his old friend Alexander Baring on 10 June 1812, expressing the hope that "for the good of all . . . the Orders in Council were recalled."[81] Girard continued with a description of his new bank and the circumstances of its inception, adding, "should you have occasion for my services in that line of Business, please to dispose of them—I intend to carry on the Establishment alluded to with prudence, Interest will only be a secondary object." With an eye toward establishing closer ties, he inquired about a possible correspondent relationship. "Please inform me of the terms of your house for transacting the Banking Business which I may from time to time place to its care adding his intention respecting the extent of credit and the conditions on which it will be granted in case I should judge it advantageous to draw of your said house in anticipation of future remittances, etc., etc." Girard expressed "no objection to the rate of interest you may fix it at four or five percent as you please but it must be reciprocal." Under such an arrangement, the resourceful Girard would be able to anticipate the repatriation of his funds that remained in London by drawing on credit extended by London's largest and most prestigious banking house.

By the time Girard's letter reached the senior Baring, a state of war existed between the United States and Great Britain. Writing from London on 28 August, Baring ventured his view of Girard's new institution. "I have long been of the opinion that such an establishment was wanted in America and could not fail of success. . . . People cannot transact business confidentially with 24 Directors they can have no facilities but such as are in a strictly negative form and are besides exposed to the jealousy and observation of their neighbors. A private Banker will be found so great a convenience that I think it probable you will have almost all the commercial houses for customers."[82] It is clear from the remainder of Baring's letter that he saw Girard's bank as simply an extension of the European merchant banking tradition. "Do you issue notes," he queried. "I presume not but content yourself with deposits and keep your own cash with one of the Great Banks as our Bankers do with the Bank of England." Baring also presumed that Girard would deal extensively in foreign exchange. "You must know," he observed, "that exchange operations require decisions and are not to be managed by a Board of Directors." With respect to Girard's question on the subject of credit, Baring assured him that "we should conduct our operations with you with the most active confidence and any bounds we might set to your operations could alone arise from considerations of convenience with respect to advances that might at any time be required. I can with a view to guide you state that as far as fifty thousand pounds it will never be inconvenient to me that you should dispose of if you see any inducement and with previous notice . . . we shall not probably object to go farther."

Baring thus conceived of Girard's bank as one whose operations were confined to discount and exchange. Such a conception viewed limited banking functions as a natural outgrowth of success in the mercantile world and as a profitable way to employ surplus capital. But Girard's bank differed from the Continental or British model in a variety of respects. Unlike the typical merchant banker of the period, his bank was not integrated into his mercantile house.[83] All transactions between Stephen Girard, merchant, and Stephen Girard's Bank were explicit and conducted in the same fashion as those between other merchants and the bank. His bank engaged in discount and exchange operations, and those of deposit and issue. Furthermore, it is doubtful that Baring appreciated the scope and size of Girard's new undertaking.

Indeed, the unique character of the Girard bank lay in its combination of the flexibility and privacy of the merchant banker with the size and range of functions characteristic of the corporate banks. Flexibility allowed Girard to adjust quickly to market conditions, raising or lowering the proportions of loans and investment or discount rates, and seizing the opportunity to initiate new functions, such as investment banking or stock brokerage. Privacy insured borrowers that only one individual knew their credit needs. As one customer wrote to Simpson in 1812, "the present administration being under the command of one private proprietor, I hope my demand will not be exposed to such difficulties as could take place in other banking institutions. . . ."[84] From its very inception, the reputation, if not the success, of Stephen Girard's Bank seemed assured.

3

War and Legislative Opposition, 1812-1814

The opening of Stephen Girard's Bank was of some concern to the established banking institutions of Philadelphia. Girard was no small interloper whose impact could be ignored but a formidable competitor whose assets averaged $2,540,175 during the first year of operation.[1] This private institution entered the financial community on a par with the largest chartered bank. Consequently on 12 June 1812 the General Committee of the Philadelphia banks met to consider "the propriety of receiving in payment or on deposit the notes of Stephen Girard who has lately established a private bank in this city." After three days of deliberations, the committee passed the following resolution: "Resolved that the Laws of the Commonwealth manifestly go to discourage, if not to prohibit, the circulation of notes of unincorporated Banks, that the precedent of receiving as money, the notes of an individual or of associated Companies not established by law would be highly dangerous as the practice once introduced might be extended to cases where there is less solidity and security than in the present instance: consequently that the said notes cannot be received either in payment or on deposit at any of the banks."[2]

Ignoring the opposition of the city banks, Girard moved quickly to establish a network of correspondents in the East. In May, contacts in Wilmington and Charleston were obtained, and in June, Baltimore and New York banks were added. In the same month, the Farmer's Bank of Lancaster became Girard's first inland correspondent, and Baring Brothers and Company of London an overseas connection. The addition of Boston in October completed the network of major cities.

Within a month of commencing operations, Girard's bank was drawn into the web of wartime Treasury financing. The Republican frugality of Jefferson, Madison, and Secretary of the Treasury Albert Gallatin had ill prepared the nation for the declaration of war on Britain in June 1812. The unwillingness to institute new taxes coupled with a substantial decline in tariff revenues during 1812 necessitated a federal loan of $11 million. Moreover, the financial resources of the New England states would prove difficult to tap because of the region's opposition to the war. This laid the burden of Treasury operations on the individuals and banks of the Middle Atlantic states. The public subscription of 1 and 2 May was unsuccessful in disposing of the entire issue, despite Gallatin's assurance that "the sums to be paid on account of . . . subscriptions should be permitted to remain in deposits in the banks making the subscription, until wanted for the public service."[3] Of the $6,118,900 subscribed, the nation's banks accounted for better than two-thirds. Gallatin parceled out the remaining stock among the major eastern cities and set out personally to place the remainder of the loan with the "moneyed institutions."

In May Secretary Gallatin was in Philadelphia and requested George Simpson to call upon him. As cashier of Stephen Girard's newly established bank, Simpson was asked if his employer was "disposed to make a large loan to the government" of not less than $500,000. Simpson's record of this meeting indicates that Gallatin asserted "that the Treasury always deposited their monies in those Banks where they obtained loans" and "that he intended to make Philadelphia the chief place of the deposit," which would be divided among the banks of the city.[4] Of more direct interest to Girard was Gallatin's promise that in the case of the loan being made, "the Officers of the Government and Receivers of Public Monies for duties or for lands sold" would be directed "to take notes of Mr. G's bank in payment. . . ." Moreover, Gallatin thought "that the making of this loan by Mr. Girard would have tendency to prevail the Legislature of Pennsylvania from taking measures to arrest the progress of Mr. Girard's Bank."[5] Regarding the other Philadelphia banks, Gallatin would, if the loan was made, "recommend to the several Banks in which the public monies are deposits to receive in payment the Notes of S. Girard's Bank and to abstain from drawing Specie from each other unless in cases of extreme necessity."

These were attractive terms indeed. If Girard's notes were accepted on a par with those of other chartered banks in payment to the government, their general acceptability would be greatly enhanced. Clearly Gallatin's assistance and influence would be extremely valuable in the impending encounter with the legislature. Finally, since all important

Philadelphia institutions now held public monies, the secretary's last proposal was tantamount to a personal recommendation that the Philadelphia banks reverse their decision on the acceptance of Girard's notes.

Simpson recommended that Girard accept Gallatin's proposal in a memo dated July 1812.[6] He also sketched the terms of the loan and the advantages that would accrue to Girard from acceptance. Girard, however, moved cautiously, demanding that his bank be placed "as respects deposits, receiving Duties, paying drafts, etc., etc. on an equal footing with any one of the Banks in the City who have loaned the same amount."[7] In a 27 July note to Gallatin, Simpson noted that as Girard's deposits and circulation increased he would be in a position to lend still more.[8]

On 3 August, Gallatin indicated substantial agreement with the conditions imposed by Girard. The sole exception was the disposition of Girard's bank as a collector of revenue bonds in Philadelphia. This function was now performed by the Bank of Pennsylvania and the Farmer's and Mechanic's Bank. However, said Gallatin, "should that arrangement be hereafter altered, I would have no objection to place a part for collection in Mr. Girard's banking house. In the mean while this can make no difficulty, as the Treasurer's Drafts on the several Banks in the same place may always be so managed as to apportion the real deposits without reference to the particular collectors."[9]

Gallatin returned to Philadelphia on 6 August to work out final arrangements, but a hitch quickly developed in the negotiations. On being informed of the results of this meeting, Girard sensed a departure from the Treasury's original position. Girard quickly instructed Simpson to "inform Mr. Albert Gallatin, that the conditions stated in my letter to you of the 27th ult. must be considered as fundamental principle on which the loan of $500,000 will be granted. . . ."[10] Gallatin was unable to satisfy Girard on all counts, and on 4 August the latter informed the secretary that the proposed loan would not be forthcoming.[11] Girard would now have to face the opposition of the Pennsylvania legislature without the assurance of Gallatin's aid.

Such opposition was not long in developing, for as the state House and Senate gathered for the 1813 session a banking bill was clearly foremost in the minds of many. Historically, banking legislation had been a matter of debate between the competing factions of Pennsylvania's large and powerful Republican majority. During the early years of the nineteenth century, rural-urban differences within the state had spawned a debate on banking legislation related to branch banks. Conservative, urban groups within the legislature refused to sanction the chartering of new banks for rural areas of the state. By 1810 the legislature recognized the credit needs of small merchants and farmers in inland regions by permitting the Bank of Pennsylvania to establish branches in Lancaster, Easton, and Pittsburgh, while the Philadelphia Bank maintained offices in Columbia, Harrisburg, and Wilkes Barre. But despite such concessions, the lawmakers soon observed in these rural areas an "unbounded thirst for independently chartered institutions . . . allied to the hopeful delusion that the chartering of banks would of itself create capital."[12] That facet of the struggle over the rechartering of the First Bank of the United States that dealt with access to credit struck a responsive chord in rural Pennsylvanians. Many had come to associate the prosperity of the cities with banks, and, that being the case, they wanted banks for themselves.[13] By the second decade of the nineteenth century, new institutions had begun to spring up all over the state, with or without a charter. "A bank by many was no longer regarded as an instrument by which the surplus wealth of capitalists could be conveniently loaned to their industrious fellow citizens," observed one contemporary foe of the new banks, "but as a mint in which money could be coined at pleasure, for those who did not possess it before."[14]

The radical-liberal wing of the Republican Party, which controlled the state legislature, was sympathetic to the demand for new charters but feared the growth of nonchartered institutions. Accordingly, on 19 March 1810 they enacted a law prohibiting unincorporated institutions or "associations" from receiving deposits or issuing notes. The same law provided, however, that nothing in the act should interfere with others "in such manner and for such purpose as hath been hitherto usual and may be legally done."[15] Previous to this "restraining act," as such legislation was generally termed, there was no power possessed by a bank which was not allowed to individuals and private associations. They could, in common, issue notes, discount notes, and receive deposits. Now the creation of money (as distinct from the mere safekeeping of it) was to be reserved to corporations authorized by the state for that purpose. "The common law right to borrow was being distinguished from the right to borrow by the issue of obligations intended to circulate as money."[16] Frustrated in this attempt to eliminate all unchartered institutions, the legislature was now prepared to replace them with a host of duly authorized institutions. Ranged against the determined lawmakers were those who supported the right of individuals to engage in the business of banking and Governor Simon Snyder, whose opposition to bank expansion was well known.

Girard had good reason to be apprehensive, for his bank, more than any other, seemed to provoke the hostility of the legislature. To those who opposed the BUS because of its credit restrictions, Girard appeared to represent a continuation of that tradition. From those who opposed large banks in general, Girard came under fire simply because the size of his operations placed him on a par with the largest of the Philadelphia banks. Legislators friendly to the chartered banks opposed Girard as unwelcome competition. Finally, Girard's banking enterprise "aroused the jealousy of the Pennsylvania government, which held blocks of the stock of the incorporated banks of the state."[17]

The opening shot in the renewed campaign against the unchartered banks was a legislative proposal to tax such institutions. If enacted, such a measure would place unchartered institutions at a serious competitive disadvantage. Girard learned of the proposal in mid-January 1813 and requested Samuel Clendenin, cashier of the Farmer's Bank of Lancaster, to relay any information he might have.[18] On 22 January Clendenin promised to forward a copy of House Bill Number 130 and added that "from a cursory view of it, I think Mr. Girard has nothing to fear of this, however, he will be a better judge when he shall have an opportunity of perusing the Bill itself."[19] Four days later, Clendenin reported a decided shift in the strategy of the legislature. A bill had been reported for establishing a general system of banking that would supersede the tax measure. The new proposal would divide the state into twenty-three districts, each of which would be entitled to a bank of a given size. Clendenin quoted his informant as saying that "should these bills pass or not . . . they are determined, at all event to stop unchartered Banks. As to Stephen Girard's Bank, if anything can be done to stop, or injure its operations, it will be done."[20] On 11 February Girard and Simpson learned that the House of Representatives had passed a bill chartering some twenty-five new banks in the state and that little opposition could be expected in the Senate.[21] The bank bill did pass the Senate, but by a margin of only one vote, 14 to 13. This was a slim margin indeed, considering that the House version had been passed by a similar vote of 42 to 41. John Connelly, a friend of Girard's and a member of the House, wrote on 5 March that the measure now required only the governor's signature to become law.[22]

Much to Girard's relief, the governor vetoed the bill. Among the reasons Snyder gave for his action were the lack of sufficient capital to establish the banks; the impact such institutions might have on the wartime finances of the commonwealth; the belief that the creation of so many influential and privileged corporations should receive the vote of an indisputable majority of the legislature; and the fear that these institutions would flood the state with paper currency. The legislature adjourned without taking further action on the subject of banking.[23]

While Girard was monitoring the deliberations of the Pennsylvania legislature, Secretary of the Treasury Gallatin was desperately seeking funds to support the flagging American military effort. On 8 February 1813, Congress authorized a loan for a sum not to exceed sixteen millions of dollars—the largest borrowing operation in the history of the new nation. Coming hard on the heels of the unsuccessful loan of 1812, battlefield reverses, and the continued opposition of the New England money interests to the war effort, the chances for its success appeared dim.

Before proceeding with a public offering, Gallatin once more attempted to tap the nation's private fortunes. He chose as an intermediary in this operation David Parish of Philadelphia, the son of a Hamburg banker, John Parish. Gallatin suggested that Parish join with Girard and John Jacob Astor and Herman LeRoy of New York in a syndicate to purchase $10 million worth of government stock. Parish, however, demurred, and the project fell through. Gallatin's disappointment was evident in a letter to Madison. "My reliance on Parish is not great," said the secretary, "he . . . positively refused to join with LeRoy and Girard and with Mr. Astor in making proposals for ten millions of the loan. I had set that going, and if it had succeeded I would not have opened the loan by subscription."[24]

Thwarted in this attempt, Gallatin announced a public subscription to take place in eleven key cities on 12 and 13 March. When the books were closed, the records indicated that only $3,956,400 of the loan was taken. Girard's bank accounted for $122,600 in subscriptions, with Girard himself taking $100,000, or nearly 27 percent of all Philadelphia sales.[25] The Treasury announced a reopening of the subscription books, this time for a full week, between 25 and 31 March. Moreover, in anticipation of another failure, Gallatin indicated that he would consider until 5 April individual proposals for taking the residue of the loan as of 1 April. Significantly, such proposals were to state not only the amount of stock that the parties wished to obtain but also "the price they will allow for the same."[26]

In light of the Treasury's obvious plight, Parish reconsidered Gallatin's suggestion of a stock-purchasing syndicate and informed the secretary, through Alexander J. Dallas, that such a syndicate could succeed where the public subscription had failed, provided conditions were right.[27] Parish's plan involved a joint sale in the United States and abroad with the cooperation of Girard, Astor, and a few other prominent merchants and bankers.

If Girard had given serious thought to becoming a party to Parish's syndicate, he was content to keep such thoughts to himself. His reply to Gallatin on the matter of a proposal was cool and noncommittal. "It would be imprudent for me to increase the sum which I have already subscribed," wrote Girard, unless the secretary of the treasury "places my establishment on the same footing as any banks of this city which will have subscribed as much as I do. Should it be otherwise, the Chartered Banks of Philadelphia will continue to refuse my Bank Notes, which would, of course, compell [*sic*] me to pay in Specie the installments of the loan as they come due, from this operation it would result, that my present solid specie capital would be changed in Certificates of the Loan and noates [*sic*] and obligations of Individuals, the consequences of which would be, that having no sufficient Specie to represent and support the Credit of my Bank Notes, their circulation would greatly decrease and compel me to reduce my banking operations to a small scale."[28] In banker's terms, Girard feared a decrease in the liquidity of his institution's assets.

Parish had been hard at work during the last two weeks of March and by the thirtieth had amassed a total of $2,964,800 in subscriptions through his own efforts and those of subcontractors.[29] When the public subscription books closed on 31 March, an additional $1,881,800 in stock had been sold, bringing the total public sales to $5,838,200. Gallatin would now have to deal with those making proposals for the remainder.

On 1 April Girard broke his official silence and indicated to Parish his disposition to facilitate the loan to the United States, but he insisted that the *quid pro quo* of his participation was recognition of his bank on an equal basis with other Philadelphia institutions. Included in this communication was a detailed proposal for subscribing to some $3 million of the loan.[30] Key provisions of Girard's proposal stipulated that funds deposited in his bank for subscriptions should remain there until needed by the Treasury and under no circumstances should be transferred to other banks. Interest on the stock was to be paid through Girard's bank "with funds which the Secretary of the Treasury of the United States will lodge in time for that purpose." Finally, Girard insisted that in making a contract for the remainder of the loan, "there must be an article which will authorise said subscribers to transfer their right or shares of said Loan subscribed by them." On 2 April Parish estimated the purchases of the syndicate he was putting together as follows:[31]

$ 1,800,000	Sundry subscriptions in Philadelphia
2,000,000	John Jacob Astor and friends
1,200,000	lists at Baltimore
1,000,000	Oliver Wolcott of New York and friends
4,000,000	Girard and myself
$10,000,000	

On Monday, 5 April, Gallatin met with Girard and Parish to consider their proposal. The two Philadelphians pledged "to take as much stock of the United States bearing interest at six percent per annum, payable quarter yearly, the stock not to be redeemable before 31st December, 1825 at the rate of eighty-eight dollars for a certificate of one hundred dollars, as aforesaid, as will amount to the sum of eight millions of dollars or to the residue of the said loan. . . ." A one-quarter percent commission was to be paid on the total amount subscribed, and arrangements regarding installments were to be worked out. The same day John Jacob Astor agreed to take "for myself and my friends in New York, two millions and fifty six thousand dollars worth of the loan" on the same terms offered by Girard and Parish.[32] The effective yield was thus set at 6.8 percent, meaning that the Treasury would be required to issue $113.64 worth of stock for each $100.00 it wished to raise.

On 6 April the final disposition of the stock was agreed upon by the parties. The total amount bid by Girard, Parish, and Astor was $10,056,000. Other parties had proposed to purchase $1,050,000, and these, together with the public subscription, totaled $16,944,200. The excess of $944,200 was subtracted from the Girard-Parish proposal, leaving $7,055,800. Of this sum, Girard and Parish each took $1,191,500, with the remaining $4,672,800 going to other subscribers. Thus was concluded what was undoubtedly the first real underwriters' syndicate for the purpose of marketing government stock. As such it represented a transition by the Treasury from the old plan of borrowing directly from banks to a more roundabout process in which institutions and individuals, including bankers, bid for the stock.[33]

Girard's report to Gallatin on the sixteenth indicated that $2,181,-112.50 had been received on account of subscriptions to the loan and that this amount was credited to the treasurer of the United States, Thomas Tucker. Payments in full amounted to $1,515,300.00, and installments came to $665,812.50.[34] The original and subsequent deposits credited to the treasurer's account as a result of the loan were:[35]

16 April	$2,181,112.50
15 May	933,312.50
15 June	459,000.00
15 July	387,625.00
14 August	388,500.00
15 September	349,500.00
15 October	630,000.00
15 November	18,750.00
	$3,166,687.50

On 27 April Parish received a draft for $17,639.50, or one-quarter percent of the $7,055,800.00, from the secretary of the treasury.[36] Commission payments were made to all subcontractors of the loan by 9 July. Table 1 is a summary of these payments.

Table 1

Commissions paid on $16 million loan of 1813

Date paid	Recipient	Stock sold	Commission
4 April 1813	Biddle and Wharton	$ 783,300	$1,958.25
4 April 1813	William Overman	398,500	996.25
4 April 1813	William J. Bell	280,000	700.00
4 April 1813	Joseph Taggert	188,000	470.00
4 April 1813	George Simpson	190,000	475.00
4 April 1813	Louis Clapier	512,000	1,280.00
4 April 1813	New York Association	1,500,000	3,750.00
19 May 1813	A. Daschkoff	100,000	250.00
9 July 1813	Stephen Girard, $\frac{1}{8}$%	3,104,000	3,880.00
9 July 1813	David Parish, $\frac{1}{8}$%	3,104,000	3,880.00

Source: SGC, II, 249 (9 July 1813).

Girard soon faced serious problems related to the $16 million loan and the attendant Treasury deposits. The account of the treasurer of the United States stood at $2,090,727.21 on 1 May 1813. However, drafts by the Treasury, beginning on 19 April, soon began to reduce this balance. As table 2 indicates, this account had fallen below one million dollars by year's end.

Table 2

Government debt at Stephen Girard's Bank, 1812–1817

Date	Total government debt	U.S. 6% of 1813	Government debt— percentage of total assets	Government debt— percentage of earning assets
1812	$ 178,925.89	$ 65,574	6.81%	22.73%
1813	290,848.83	318,108	5.85	—
1814	1,394,679.82	1,245,227	40.85	67.69
1815	1,585,822.27	1,431,276	40.68	74.53
1816	1,137,427.61	1,132,578	23.86	45.16
1817	1,021,331.94	1,016,882	28.36	46.42

Source: SGC, III, 94, and SGC, II, 393–94.

Part of the agreement between Girard and Gallatin at the time the loan was negotiated involved the handling of drafts on Girard's bank. Agents of the Treasury were to present drafts to Girard's bank, whereupon an account would be opened in the agent's name. The latter was then to make payments by writing checks on that account. The real threat to Girard's operations was posed by the possibility that a draft would end up in the hands of a rival Philadelphia bank. Should an agent of the government utilize a Treasury draft to open an account at a rival bank, that institution would acquire a claim on Stephen Girard's Bank which was payable in specie. Since hundreds of thousands of dollars in such drafts were presented monthly, the problem was of great concern to Girard. Thus the understanding between Gallatin and Girard concerning the disposition of Treasury drafts was crucial to the integrity of the latter's banking operations.

But Gallatin was no longer at the Treasury. He left for Europe in early May to join a team of American negotiators seeking peace with Britain, leaving Secretary of the Navy William Jones as acting secretary of the treasury. Girard moved quickly to establish relations with the new secretary. On his part, Jones assured Girard that "the Agents of the Navy Department have been already, and those of the War Department will be immediately instructed to open accounts with your Bank for all sums received in drafts upon it; and their payments will consequently be made by means of checks drawn in favor of the persons to whom those payments are made, upon your Bank. . . ."[37]

Despite the assurances, Girard dispatched Parish to Washington to sound out the acting secretary and safeguard their combined interests. On 25 May the Bank of Pennsylvania presented Girard with a draft for $15,000.00 in favor of William Leonard, deputy quartermaster.[38] This prompted Girard to take matters into his own hands. Drawing on his large stock of Philadelphia bank notes, he presented the Bank of Pennsylvania with $100,000.00 in their own notes. When the bank offered in return a combination of drafts, obligations, and notes of Stephen Girard's Bank amounting to $96,989.06, the infuriated Girard ordered Simpson to present still another $200,000.00 in notes to the same bank. "I do not intend to embarass any one of our Banks," Girard told Parish, "but as they have agreed among themselves not to take my notes, it is not reasonable to suppose that I will be so accommodating as to retain theirs as a Relick, and to turn out the Solid means of my Banking Establishment, particularly at a moment when prudence dictates, that I should at all times have a Sufficient Specie in my Bank to meet the Debts of that Establishment." Girard instructed Parish to make it clear that his tactics were defensive in nature and suggested bypassing Jones to seek the intervention of higher office. "If you have the opportunity to converse with the President of the United States and with the Secretary of War," said Girard, "please to say something respecting the conditions upon which you and me have taken the residue of the Loan. If the funds resulting therefrom are constantly taken from my Bank to be lodged in others, it will seriously derange my operations particularly at a moment when money Men who expect a new Loan is wanted, will not be disposed to purchase stock from us."[39]

To understand Girard's concern it is necessary to appreciate the extent of his involvement in the Treasury's debt. As table 2 indicates, Girard's holdings of all kinds of government debt grew nearly fivefold between 1813 and 1814 and comprised over 40 percent of total assets in 1814 and 1815. Virtually the entire increase in government debt holdings during these years was a result of participation in the $16 million loan. Moreover, government debt as a proportion of *earning* assets grew to two-thirds in 1814 and three-fourths in 1815.

Should the market for government stock turn sour, Girard's bank could face a liquidity crisis of substantial proportions. Jones's reaction to the specie raid on the Bank of Pennsylvania did little to calm Girard's anxiety. The secretary indicated that he understood perfectly well that government deposits were to stay in Girard's bank in order "to shield . . . against the attack of the incorporated Banks. . . ."[40] However, he continued, it is the practice of the Treasury to "direct the monied operations of the public to the preservation of credit, by maintaining the equilibrium between the monied institutions of the country and as it protected your institution by the management alluded to, so will it guard those institutions against any undue pressure which the public funds in your vaults may enable you to direct against them." Futhermore, warned Jones, the continuance of such raids "will induce the prompt application of a specific remedy." A hint of such "specific remedies" was included in Jones's letter of 28 May. He stated that contrary to expectations, "it will be impossible to apply to the public service in Philadelphia, all the monies paid and payable on account of the loan into your Bank. . . ."[41] Since the Girard-Gallatin agreement was based on the guarantee that all funds would be spent in Philadelphia, this new development raised the possibility of substantial specie claims on Girard's bank by out-of-state institutions. Worse still, if such banks were correspondents of other Philadelphia institutions, specie raids on Girard could continue.

Girard decided to retreat from his position and so informed Parish. "Although I believe that I am correct," said Girard, "yet wishing to avoid displeasing the acting Secretary of the Treasury, I have decided to stop the drawing of Specie. . . . I beg that you will endeavor to Sponge off any unjust impressions."[42] Parish was relieved at Girard's decision and reported that Jones appeared anxious for the feud between Girard and the chartered banks of Philadelphia to cease. While the secretary "does not think that it would be proper for him to interfere in his official capacity," said Parish, ". . . he will probably write a private letter or two to his friends in your City expressive of his opinion on that Subject."[43] In return for his cooperation, Girard was allowed some discretion in designating the out-of-state banks to which Treasury drafts would be presented.[44] In addition, anticipating the need to use drafts in the District of Columbia, Jones warned Girard that the Bank of Washington and the Bank of Columbia both had strong ties with Philadelphia banks, and drafts presented there would most likely end up in the hands of Girard's antagonists. Therefore, said Jones, such drafts will "not be drawn upon you unless necessary; and you will be advised of it."[45]

Despite his useful liaison work in Washington, Parish's relations with Girard rapidly deteriorated during the summer of 1813. Parish had arranged to borrow the funds for his first installment from Girard on very favorable terms. As subsequent installments came due, Girard was time and again compelled to advance funds for his partner's share. By 27 July Parish had borrowed $595,750.00 to pay four installments of $148,937.50 each. On 14 August an additional $148,937.50 was advanced by Girard, and a like amount on 15 September. Finally, on 15 October cash was advanced to Parish in the sum of $297,875.00. Thus the entire $1,191,500.00 subscription was financed by Girard.[46] In order to meet Parish's obligations, Girard was forced to curtail the operations of his bank. By June the drafts issued by the Treasury Department on Girard's bank began to exceed the payments on the loan, thus reducing the Treasury balances. This factor was complicated by the specie raids engineered by the Bank of Pennsylvania and others. Girard reminded Parish in October that "after the payment of the Second Installment circumstances rendered advisable to take every precautionary step to meet the drafts of the Treasury for that purpose I reduced my discounts, sold 6 percent Stock and even Bills on England. Although you were at that time informed of that circumstance you did not appear to make any arrangements for the reimbursement of the two installments which I had paid for you."[47] Although Girard had originally specified that the loan was to be interest free, he began charging 4 percent against the unpaid balance on 15 July. Interest charges amounted to $2,410.31 between that date and 18 October, when Parish finally settled his accounts with Girard.[48]

On 24 October Parish reminded Girard that when he had entered into the joint loan operation "it was under a full expectation that the benefit of the arrangement I made for you with Mr. Gallatin, would be extended to me for my share of the Loan, as long as it did not subject you to loss—that is to say—I was not to pay interest as long as funds remain in your Bank resulting from payments made towards the Loan. . . ."[49] Moreover, Parish claimed a share of any profits arising out of the bank's large Treasury deposits. Girard, of course, was adamant on this point. He replied that "in regard to the funds belonging to the United States and others which are deposited in my Bank they shall at all times be at the disposal of their owners and should there be any advantage resulting from the confidence which the public or individuals have placed in that Institution, a Gentleman who has no funds therein and does not contribute towards its various expenses cannot expect to participate in its profits."[50] On this discordant note, Girard abruptly ended the affairs of the syndicate formed in April and turned his attention once again to external attacks on his bank.

There was, of course, the virtual certainty that the Pennsylvania legislature would renew its attempt to eliminate unchartered institutions. Before this materialized, however, problems rose in another quarter. On 2 August 1813 the Congress passed "an act laying duties on notes of banks, bankers and certain companies, on notes, bonds and obligations discounted by banks, bankers and certain companies, and on bills of exchange of certain descriptions." While principally a wartime revenue measure, this bill nonetheless contained one important provision that affected unincorporated banks. The rate of taxation was set at 1 percent on a bank's total note issue, but incorporated banks could, if they so desired, pay an annual composition of 1½ percent of dividends in lieu of the tax. Private institutions, since they issued no dividends, had no choice but to pay the bank-note tax. The tax was to be paid by having the bank's unsigned notes stamped by the Treasury prior to issue. Thus banks paying the tax on notes were liable for all notes issued, whether or not they were in circulation. The federal tax was scheduled to go into effect on 1 January 1814. On 27 December 1813 Girard informed William Jones at the Treasury that "in conformity with the law of the United States laying duty on Banks I have applied to Tench Coxe Esq. and represented to him, that as I am a private Banker transacting business with my own Capital, the neat result of my operation is without reverse versed half-yearly into the Capital Stock and consequently cannot be considered as a dividend which is distributed to the stockholders. . . . I have proposed to pay . . . the duty alluded to, on the Girard added that Coxe had eschewed responsibility in the matter and neat amount of the Discount which will be made in my Bank. . . ."[51]

had urged him to petition the Treasury directly. Jones replied that he would refer the matter to William Pinkney, the attorney general, for an opinion. On 3 January Jones sent Girard a copy of Pinkney's opinion, "by which it will be perceived that . . . the Secretary of the Treasury is not authorized to make such agreement."[52] Girard quickly replied that he would "immediately act in conformity hoping that a change in the law on the Subject of Duty on Bank notes will place me on the footing of others."[53]

The matter was of some concern to Girard, as a few simple calculations will indicate. Girard's net profits for 1814 were approximately $68,000.00. The composition on these would amount to a tax liability of $1,020.00. Alternatively, Girard's bank-note issue *averaged* $693,806.00 for the year 1814, which at 1 percent implied a tax of $6,938.06.

Girard enlisted the assistance of Alexander J. Dallas, Jared Ingersoll, the attorney general of Pennsylvania, and his son Charles J. Ingersoll, congressman from Philadelphia and chairman of the House Judiciary Committee, to persuade the House and Senate to make an exception in his case. Despite the careful drafting of a memorial by Dallas and the elder Ingersoll and the passage of a relief bill in the House, the Senate, by a vote of 11 to 10, failed to pass the exemption. On 13 April 1814, Charles J. Ingersoll wrote, "I am sorry to inform you that the Senate have just negatived the bill sent from this home for placing your banking establishment on a footing with all others as respects commutation under the Stamp Act."[54] Girard had lost another battle in the struggle to obtain official recognition of his bank on the same legal basis as the state-chartered institutions.

The stamp tax measure was a minor problem compared to the renewed attack of the Pennsylvania legislature on unincorporated banks. Here was an issue that threatened the very existence of his new institution. Yet in the end, the basic conflict between Girard and the state legislature lay in their different views of the role of the individual entrepreneur and the corporation within the legal and economic framework of the day. The Banking Act of 1814, which was ultimately passed despite Girard's best efforts, was never seriously applied to Stephen Girard's Bank.

As in the preceding year, the first indication of the proceedings at Harrisburg came from Samuel Clendenin, the erstwhile cashier of the Farmer's Bank of Lancaster. "From what I can learn," said Clendenin, "the framers aim a deadly blow at all individuals and associations who may now or may hereafter Bank without a special Act of Incorporation."[55] Girard marshaled his forces for the encounter that was sure to ensue. On 7 January 1814 he addressed a letter to Governor Snyder in which he reminded the chief executive that on 23 May 1812 he had clearly stated his intention to start a bank and petitioned Snyder for protection as far as he would judge "lawful and reasonable."[56] Girard's other chief associates in this lobbying effort were Charles Biddle and John Connelly, members of the legislature from Philadelphia; Benjamin Morgan, his principal lobbyist; and, behind the scenes, Alexander J. Dallas, his long-time friend and legal advisor.

The cornerstone of Girard's case was a memorial drafted for him by Dallas and presented to the legislature by Biddle on 13 January.[57] As this document indicates, Girard viewed the proposed banking legislation as more than an attempt to exert control over note-issuing institutions. There was the broader question of corporate and individual rights under law and custom. It is perhaps a truism that while banking in Europe had its origin in a surplus of financial capital, in America it was the product of a scarcity of accumulated savings. The practical result of this difference was significant. In Europe the tradition of the individual banker or the private banking house based on accumulated wealth was well established. The failure of such a tradition to develop in the United States was primarily traceable to the capital limitations of individual enterprise in this area. American economic conditions required credit institutions of a size that excluded individual participation of all but the very wealthy, and even among this select group there were few who ventured into the field of private commercial banking. Some banks were formed on a limited partnership basis as a substitute for incorporation, but such ventures were not numerically significant. Ironically, the strong philosophical commitment to the laissez-faire philosophy and the glorification of unincorporated enterprise in other areas contrasted sharply with a vigorous crusade against unincorporated enterprise in banking. "There was much talk expressing 'decided approbation' of the unchartered enterprises; there was more defending them. A defense of their position was not even forthcoming from the unchartered entrepreneurs themselves, who, especially as their business expanded, sought desperately some emancipation from the liability obligations their status imposed."[58]

As in so many other matters, Girard was a conspicuous exception to the rule. He sought no emancipation from the burden of his liabilities but instead worked diligently to increase them. Eschewing the protection of a corporate charter and the limited liability it bestowed, he asserted the right to employ his capital as he saw fit. To Girard the confidence which the public placed in his institution was a sufficient indication of his right to stand alongside the most prestigious chartered institutions of the day.

The general provisions of "An Act Regulating Banking," which was

under debate in January 1814, divided the commonwealth of Pennsylvania into twenty-seven districts and allowed for the chartering of a pro-
portionate number of banks in each district.[59] The first provision declared
all unincorporated banks unlawful; the second rendered null and void
all "orders and notes payable to bearer or order, in the manner, or
nature of Bank notes" issued by any individual or corporation not
incorporated for banking purposes; and the third declared that any
person or persons who issued the above instruments should be deemed
an "unlawful Bank" within the preceding section.[60]

Girard's objections to the act were carefully channeled into two
categories. The first was a constitutional argument based on general
principles and the rights of the individual under law. The second was
a more pragmatic attempt to establish the usefulness and legitimacy of
his establishment. In the constitutional approach, Girard argued that the
banking act would "deprive him of the immediate enjoyment of his
rights" and "impair the Constitutional Security of every citizen for
Property and credit the Legitimate (although not constant) rewards of
industry and integrity." The bill, maintained Girard, "places the civil
rights of an individual citizen" derived from the Constitution upon the
same footing "with the artificial rights of a Corporation, created by
legislative grant.[61] While it has been the policy of the government to
declare unlawful *voluntary associations* for the purpose of banking, it
has treated individual banks on the same footing with the farmer,
mechanic, manufacturer, etc."[62] Moreover, the memorial declares that
"the power of government relative to corporations affords no analogy to
justify an interposition with the industrious, honest pursuits of an
Individual Citizen." While the legislature may withhold such rights, the
individual citizen has "neither the reason to acquire nor the capacity to
enjoy" such rights, for he has them inherently. This ringing, affirmation
of individual rights was in the best tradition of Jeffersonian Republi-
canism and would have provoked little opposition from the legislature
in any area other than banking.

Girard saw no special merit in the concept of limited liability. Noting
that most banks chartered were founded on what he termed "limited
responsibility," he pointed out that such action "would probably be
regarded by every intelligent and candid mind as a measure impairing
at once the security of the Public and the rights of the Citizen." Observ-
ing that charters were often granted for a price (that is, payment of a
bonus to the granting legislature) and that the government was a principal stockholder in many banks, Girard maintained that the rights of individuals should not be sacrificed for a public or semipublic monopoly.[63]

Furthermore, Girard maintained that institutions that were taxed equally were equal before the law. As an individual engaged in the banking business, Girard noted that he paid both state and federal taxes. Indeed, he observed, "the late Acts of Congress impose . . . a tax upon the operations of Banks, whether they are conducted by individuals, by companies or by corporations."[64]

Finally, Girard's memorial maintained that the bank bill would violate his constitutional rights as a Pennsylvania citizen. The Constitution "guards as an inherent and indefeasible right acquiring, possessing and protecting property." In addition, noted Girard, the state constitution forbade ex post facto laws and laws imparing contracts. Other non-chartered institutions had used the ex post facto argument to escape the terms of previous banking legislation. Clearly, Girard was aware of this strategy, for in November 1813 he instructed his cashier to warn Jonathan Burrall, cashier of the Bank of America, about the Commercial Bank of Philadelphia. "The Commercial Bank," said Simpson, "is not chartered and the restricting Law of this State is very severe against such associations. They pretend that their operations commenced prior to the passing of said Law and that consequently they are not subject to its penaltys."[65]

In a more practical vein, Girard argued that on the basis of merit and performance alone his establishment was justified. "The lawfulness of the Institution . . . was affirmed by the opinion of learned Council, its design was communicated to the Governor of the state, in the Month of May, 1812: and its operations commenced in the succeeding month of June under every practical arrangement that could be desired for the security and accommodation of its customers. Experience of Eighteen Months, has tested the principals of this Institution [and] has fixed its reputation upon the base of public confidence." As for the public, "every Citizen fairly entitled to Credit has found it there for a period of lending considerably beyond the usual periods of Discount." This was the case, added Girard, whether the borrower was a merchant, farmer, mechanic, or manufacturer and whether the loan was for private use, business use, or for the completion of turnpike roads and other public works. This description sharply contrasts with the bank's actual practice, which was to lend on a short-term basis for strictly commercial purposes.

Girard even attempted to capitalize on his recent role in the $16 million federal loan of 1813 by pointing out that the Treasury of the United States had found that his bank invited "the strictest inquiry under the Legislative authority into the principles and practice of the Institution."

Summing up Girard's position, it seems fair to say that he was not opposed to governmental intervention in the area of banking; he was, after all, a key figure in the establishment of the Second Bank of the

United States. Rather, he objected to the transfer to corporations of what he considered inherent, individual rights to the exclusion of private citizens engaged in the same business. On the other hand, if the government—state or federal—was to accept its responsibilities regarding the supply of money and credit, the transfer of such rights and responsibilities was necessary. In the area of commercial banking, the Republican regard for government nonintervention did not carry the day. The control formerly exerted by Hamilton's much maligned national bank was to be replaced by the Republican-inspired banking laws of the commonwealth.

Despite Benjamin Morgan's assessment that Girard's memorial had "made a serious impression on many of the members," he did not expect that the "progress of the bill" could "be asserted in the house of representatives or altered in any just conformity with the constitution, justice and your Interest and wishes. Of the Senate," added Morgan, "I entertain better expectations and am daily, nay hourly, with its members with whom no efforts should and none I can make during my stay here shall be spared."[66] Morgan's view proved to be essentially accurate. John Connelly reported that the whole of the 18 January session was taken up with discussion of an amendment to strike out the word "individuals" in the seventh and tenth lines of the bill. Having failed in this Connelly proposed an amendment to the eleventh section of the bill, excluding Girard from the penalty of the act during the war and for twelve months after a treaty of peace was concluded between Great Britain and the United States. This strategy also failed. "This is the last effort which Mr. Duane or myself will make to amend this bill," lamented Connelly, "hence I consider it as having passed this house for there is not one else to oppose it. How the Senate may dispose of the Bill is yet uncertain."[67]

Faced with the probability of the bill's passage, Girard explored the possibility of obtaining a charter. He instructed Connelly "to make such arrangements as you will judge advisable on the principle that the capital of my Bank will not exceed $1,500,000. Should you be of the opinion that the legislature wishes to charter my Bank under the name of Stephen Girard & Co. Bank . . . you may agree to a bonus of about 5 percent on capital of $1,500,000. . . . On the subject of a yearly tax," added Girard, "I think that the sum should be less than three percent which may be imposed on the dividends of the New Bank except I should be placed on their footing as it respects the privileges which are attached to a charter."[68]

By the end of January the passage of the bank bill was certain, and Girard permitted himself an opinion on the law. "First," he noted, "those in favor of the Bank Bill will state that it is designed to protect the public from individuals with insufficient means for establishing a bank." Second, such a bill is designed to protect associations formed to do banking business from unchartered competition. The latter, said Girard, could be corrected by proper legislation. As to the former, "no man will establish a Bank of his own without he has sufficient funds, good credit, and a great share of public confidence otherwise he will soon be compelled to shut up."[69] In short, the operation of the market place would discourage those of less than adequate means from establishing banks in the first place and quickly eliminate those who refused to be discouraged. In the eyes of the legislature, however, the question was not whether the market mechanism would operate to eliminate upstart institutions, but whether such a mechanism was appropriate to the banking sector. The concept was gaining support that the success or failure of banks was too important a matter to be left entirely to the dictates of the market place.

Much to everyone's surprise, the Senate defeated the bank bill by a vote of 17 to 13. However, as Morgan warned, any two members of the majority could move a reconsideration of the vote within six weeks.[70] A motion to reconsider was defeated on 11 February, but the motion of 15 February was successful. "The Friends of the late horrid Banking Bill," wrote Samuel Clendenin, "have succeeded in calling it up again in the Senate."[71] A motion to postpone the action of the bill on Girard's bank until January 1815 was carried, but so was the bill. Governor Snyder once again vetoed the bank bill, but this time he was overridden and the bill became law on 21 March 1814. "This has been effected by the influence of moneyed associations against the rights of the people," said John Connelly. "I consider this as an entering wedge to a system that will change the present order of things and bring disgrace upon the state."[72]

In principle Girard had lost his struggle. In practice, however, the state was lenient in its treatment of his institution. When the first of the year arrived, Stephen Girard's Bank was posted as illegal at Harrisburg, but no action was taken by the authorities. On 12 February 1815, Girard wrote to Simon Snyder that "knowing your friendly disposition towards that class of citizens, whose conduct merits the approbation and protection of government, I take the liberty to inform you that although I have complied with the Law passed by the Legislature of the State on the subject of Private Bankers, yet I had the mortification to observe my name at the head of several others published as an unlawful Bank at the Seat of Government."[73] A short but pointed exchange of letters with the commonwealth banking authorities resulted in the deletion of Girard's name from the list.[74]

The winter of 1814 saw the end of William Jones's tenure as acting secretary of the treasury and the appointment of George W. Campbell

4

Suspension and The Bank
of the United States, 1814-1819

By the late summer of 1814 the banks of the Atlantic seaboard were prepared to embrace a radical solution to their problems. During the spring and summer the drain of specie had been especially heavy. In particular, New England banks insisted on specie payments for the Treasury drafts that they held. Much of this specie was drawn from the New York banks, but these institutions, in turn, called on their Philadelphia correspondents to replenish their supplies. In the case of Stephen Girard's Bank, 1814 saw frequent demands for specie on the part of the Bank of America in New York. It was small consolation to Girard and Simpson that no sooner did the Bank of America acquire such specie than it continued its flow toward Boston.

Girard's specie supply fell from $896,311.41 on 1 January 1814 to $174,143.47 by 1 April of the same year.[1] This forced a sharp contraction of loans, which plummeted from over one million dollars on 1 April to a low of $611,486.83 on 1 July.[2] The chartered banks of Philadelphia, faced with similar conditions, held a series of joint bank committee meetings between 26 August and 29 August. On the latter date a document was circulated in Philadelphia entitled an "Open Notice to Banks" and signed "A Friend to Public Credit."[3] Actually written by Mathew Carey, this document clearly presented the alternatives open to the beleaguered banks of the city. As Carey saw matters, the solutions quickly reduced to two: first, a further curtailment of loans and discounts, with the attendant devastating impact on the nation's economy, and second, a general suspension of specie payments. Carey advocated

45

suspension and commented that "it saved England from bankruptcy and has been recently tried and found adequate to its object at New Orleans." Moreover, added Carey, "within a month it will no longer be a matter of choice . . . the refusal of one or two Banks to unite in this measure, ought not to prevent the others from adopting it. The Bank that longest refuses to accede will suffer the most inconvenience." On the same date there was a unique joint meeting of bank boards, and the decision to suspend was announced. The response of the commercial community was immediate, and "at a well attended meeting of merchants and traders held at the Merchants' Coffee House on August 31, 1814, a resolution was unanimously adopted approving the suspension and agreeing to receive in payment of all debts . . . the notes of the said banks."[4]

The quantitative impact of suspension on Girard's bank was immediate and immense. Although not a party to the agreements worked out by the other city banks, Girard was forced to follow their lead in the process of retrenchment. Table 3 tells the story. Total loans continued

Table 3

Economic indicators of suspension of specie payments at Stephen Girard's Bank

Date		Total loans	Bank notes in circulation	Deposits (individual)	Deposits by other banks	Loan/asset ratio
1812	1	$ —	$ —	$ —	$ —	—
	2	715,927	—	174,397	152,813	—
	3	749,371	—	294,751	115,126	18.27
	4	941,624	—	472,627	404,655	35.56
1813	1	1,588,054	—	489,688	—	38.67
	2	1,948,416	—	—	—	—
	3	1,027,392	—	—	—	—
	4	1,144,068	—	626,867	—	27.80
1814	1	1,235,229	—	565,997	—	43.45
	2	625,887	191,870	529,359	—	24.86
	3	683,035	110,730	566,669	—	19.58
	4	325,121	232,485	520,226	—	13.00
1815	1	310,254	136,237	461,800	50,089	8.32
	2	555,975	151,302	526,871	61,038	13.55
	3	583,725	271,887	673,534	70,113	13.90
	4	818,832	323,100	635,079	36,490	20.42

Source:　SGC, II, 393.

to fall and eventually reached a low of $310,253.83 in the first quarter of 1813. Bank notes in circulation fell to an all-time low in the third quarter of 1814; however, individual deposits held their own throughout 1814–1815. The decline in business and interbank clearings is reflected in the level of deposits by other banks. In Girard's case, these were all out-of-town banks, and the sharp decline reflects a decrease in interregional transactions. Finally, the loan/asset ratio stood at a dismal 8.32 percent by the first quarter of 1815.

Girard was not the only one to feel the pressure from suspension. Secretary of the Treasury Campbell had been under great strain since assuming office, and the decision by all but the New England banks to suspend specie payments proved to be a fatal blow. Campbell's ineptitude in managing the nation's finances convinced the administration that new leadership was required. In September, Dallas indicated to Monroe his willingness to accept the Treasury post and the administration responded favorably. Even the radical Republicans were now prepared to accept Dallas' nomination.

Two days before his nomination, set for 5 October, Dallas wrote to Girard requesting his advice on the "enclosed sketch"—a plan for a national bank. Dallas had been active, along with Girard, Astor, and Parish, in an attempt to bring the issue of a national bank before the Congress in the spring of 1814. Although that attempt had failed, Dallas was now in a position to exert considerably more influence in the matter. Dallas' sketch envisioned a bank with capital of $50 million, owned by the government (40 percent) and the public (60 percent), with a thirty-year charter. One-tenth of the $30 million public subscription would consist of gold or silver coin, and nine-tenths of coin or government stock issued since the declaration of war. Of the fifteen directors, the president was to appoint five and the stockholders to elect ten, with voting in proportion to the number of shares held. The bank could be required to make 6 percent loans to the federal government, and its notes would be acceptable in payment of debts to the government.[5]

Girard's comments were generally concerned with protecting the interests of current bondholders and future stockholders of the proposed bank.[6] One of his suggestions, which was eventually incorporated in the BUS charter, was that the bank should not be permitted to dump large amounts of 6 percent stock on the market without prior notice to the secretary of the treasury.[7] Another suggestion, which was not eventually adopted, would have prevented the government from selling its shares in the bank before the charter ran out. Such self-serving suggestions prompted Daniel Webster to assess the eventual plan adopted for a national bank as "a project calculated only for the benefit of the holders of the stock issued since the war."[8]

Dallas had been in office less than two weeks when he suggested that Girard renew his petition to Congress regarding the stamp tax on bank notes. "Upon reflection," noted Dallas, "it would not be proper to originate with me."[9] Girard quickly complied, submitting on 24 October virtually the same memorial that had been drafted by Dallas the preceding January.[10] This time the relief act experienced smooth sailing in both House and Senate. On 8 December Senator Roberts of Pennsylvania informed Girard that the measure had passed both houses and needed only the signatures of the speaker of the house, the president of the senate, and President Madison to become law.[11] The bill was signed into force on 10 December 1814. In the eyes of the federal government, Girard's bank was to be placed on the same footing with the same options as the incorporated institutions.

In light of the suspension of specie payments by most of the nation's banks, the matter of establishing a new national bank took on a greater urgency. Dallas kept Girard informed of the bank's progress and sought his advice frequently. Reporting the support of the House Ways and Means Committee for his plan, Dallas added, "It is a source of great satisfaction to me that I can have perfect confidence in your aid as a friend and patriot."[12]

David Parish left for Washington on 22 October and reported a week later to Girard that he found a "majority in both houses of Congress are unquestionably in favor of the measure."[13] Both House and Senate committees at work on the bank bill reported out versions that significantly reduced the government's role in its operations. Calhoun, Webster, and other opponents appeared to be determined to amend the bank bill to death if possible. The government was now asked to give up its right to name directors and to reduce its share of ownership to $10 million. "Without these alterations," reported Parish, "not a federal vote will be obtained in favor of the Bank and without some aid from that side of the house the bill will not pass as many democrats are opposed to it on constitutional grounds."[14]

Some were opposed not to the bank per se but to the purpose they perceived it was to serve. This faction (led by Calhoun in the Senate) viewed the bank as an administration scheme to borrow needed funds by the inflationary process of printing bank notes. They also raised the question of whether sufficient specie existed to purchase the bank's capital stock. Moreover, what would happen to the bank's specie reserves if it stood ready to redeem its notes in gold and silver while all the banks around it did not?

Such concerns existed among private bankers as well. In a letter to George Simpson, Jonathan Burrall of the Bank of America expressed doubt that a sufficient amount of specie could be raised, and predicted that even if it was it would soon disappear as the new bank's notes were returned for payment in gold and silver. Burrall also expressed the fear that governmental needs might induce the bank to issue notes in excess of the need for a circulating medium. The state banks, he said, will either accept the national bank notes, which will become a major part of their capital, or pay them out, in which case they will replace the state notes as circulating medium. Fearing that the operation of a bank now would be "throwing away *a good thing*," he viewed such an institution instead as an effective instrument for reviving the credit of bank notes and funded debt immediately after the war, "when it could commence with paying specie and continue to do so." A bank at the present time, he predicted, would simply add to the supply of depreciated currency and hinder the return to specie payments.[15] In essence, this point of view raised the question that was to haunt proponents and opponents of the bank for the next two years—could a national bank be successfully established apart from a plan to resume specie payments by the state banks?

In November the House bill was rejected by the Congress, prompting Girard to react. "I am extremely sorry," he told Charles Ingersoll, "that the House of Representatives have not adopted Mr. Dallas' Plan of a National Bank; it is to be regretted that jealousy or some other sinister cause against the class of wealthy citizens who have loaned their money to Government will induce gentlemen to reject the best mode of consolidating the Credit of the United States, an event which alone can force an honorable Peace."[16]

Revived by the Senate and passed in December, still another bank bill was defeated in the House.[17] Supporters of the bank were able to carry a move to reconsider the bill, and the issue was sent back to committee. The bill that emerged easily passed the House on 7 January and the Senate on 20 January. However, opponents had successfully gutted the original proposal, so that Madison held the bill for ten days and then, on the advice of Dallas, vetoed it. On 18 February the unhappy secretary of the treasury wrote to Girard, "It is mortifying to tell you that no Bank will be established during the present session of Congress."[18]

Some urgency was removed from the issue of the banks with the arrival of news on 13 February 1814 that a peace treaty with Britain had been concluded at Ghent. Notwithstanding the conclusion of hostilities, the last year of the war had been a most embarrassing period for the Treasury. The public debt had not been paid punctually, and Treasury notes had been routinely dishonored. "So completely empty was the Treasury and destitute of credit that funds could not be obtained to defray the current ordinary expenses of the different Departments. Disgraceful, humiliating, as the fact was . . . the Department of State was so bare of money as to be unable to pay even its stationery bill. It was well known to the citizens of the District that the Treasury was obliged to borrow pitiful sums which it would disgrace a merchant in tolerable credit to ask for. . . ."[19] In an effort to remedy the situation, Dallas quickly moved to establish better relations with the nation's banks. In February and March 1815, the secretary tried to convince Girard and others that they should participate in a scheme that would "connect the prosperity of such of the State Banks, as are deserving of confidence, with the fiscal operations of the government" and release "every part of the community" from the acute embarrassments "which the want of a competent circulating medium has produced."[20]

Girard was in no mood, however, for such an arrangement and made this clear to Dallas. A large portion of Girard's energies during this period were devoted to re-establishing his world-wide trade network. With foreign commerce no longer threatened by the Royal Navy or legislative prohibitions, he could devote less time to banking. Despite such distractions, however, Girard was always alert to the possibility of improving his bank's position. In April 1815 he hit upon a scheme that was mutually beneficial to his bank and the Treasury.

Dallas was experiencing difficulty in transferring Treasury funds from banks in the South to northern cities where payments to the government's creditors were due. Girard offered to employ John Stoney, his Charleston connection, to obtain a transfer of such funds. The Bank of South Carolina would collect Treasury drafts for Dallas, the proceeds of which would be credited to Girard's account at that institution. Girard would then credit an equivalent amount to the Treasury account at his bank in Philadelphia. As a result, Dallas would have funds to draw upon in Philadelphia, and Girard could utilize the Charleston credits to purchase depreciated Treasury notes in the South. Because of this arrangement, the Treasury account at Girard's bank, which had dwindled to $38.00 by 1 January 1815, began to rise rapidly. Between that date and 24 June, some $504,798.41 was added to the Treasury account and $65,000.00 expended, leaving a 1 July balance of $439,836.51.[21]

Girard now felt that the time was ripe to obtain additional favors from the Treasury. In an effort to bolster the acceptability of Treasury obligations in Philadelphia, Girard informed Dallas of his intention "to receive Treasury notes with interest accrued drawn in payment and on deposit, in like manner [as] Bank notes are rec'd in S.G.'s Bank."[22] This was a generous offer, considering that such notes were exchanging below par in Philadelphia. In return for this favor, however, Dallas was to make Girard's bank a depository for the federal reserves.[23] Dallas felt obliged to accede in this matter. The collectors of imposts and international duties were ordered to deposit in Girard's bank their Treasury notes and a proportion of their deposits of money collected for duties. As of 18 June, noted Girard, the collector of the port had deposited Treasury notes amounting to $47,120.00, plus $1,078.41 interest, for a total of $48,198.41. "I am much flattered with the confidence which you are please [*sic*] to place in that Banking Establishment," wrote Girard, "and beg that you will accept my thanks for that mark of attention."[24] On 1 July, Girard informed Nicholas Kern, the collector of the revenue in Philadelphia, that in addition to Treasury notes and specie, his bank would receive for deposit the bank notes of Boston, New York, Trenton, Camden, New Brunswick, the Bank of Delaware, the Bank of Reading and Germantown, Pennsylvania, and the banks of Philadelphia city and the Northern Liberties.[25]

Girard's success in obtaining for his bank the deposits of government revenues marked a high point in the campaign for official recognition that he had launched three years earlier. The results of Dallas' efforts, however, were a marked contrast to Girard's success. The secretary was still struggling with the problems of federal financing, establishing an acceptable circulating medium, and the resumption of specie payments. By October 1815, Dallas had given up the idea of achieving resumption through a voluntary arrangement between the Treasury and the banks. The secretary sought advice from Girard on the best manner of proceeding. Girard claimed no reluctance to return to a specie standard. He boasted that "I will cheerfully give the necessary instructions so that the operations of my banking establishment may be conducted conformably to any plan which will be adopted by one or two of the oldest Banks of this City for the purpose of resuming Specie payments."[26] However, Girard expressed reservations concerning the payment of specie for the notes of other banks deposited in his institution. Holdings of such notes had increased dramatically from $651,807.00 on 1 July 1814 to $1,325,278.03 on 1 October 1815.[27] "As it respects that class of creditors who have claims on Banks for deposits of Notes issued by other Banks I do not place these on the same footing as the Bearers of Bank Notes and I am inclined to believe that the former cannot expect to receive in payment a different kind of money than what they have deposited for their own convenience. . . ." According to Girard, the banks of Philadelphia and the vicinity had "a pretty considerable amount of Bank notes in circulation owing principally to the impossibility of obtaining punctual payment for the promissory notes or other obligations which they have liberally discounted or renewed," and, he added,

"I am informed that the Banks of New York and Baltimore are in the same situation."[28]

Dallas felt that banks should either pay specie for their notes or pay interest on them. Girard, however, was quick to point out that resumption itself was not sufficient to restore the system to its former state. "All prudent and solid Banks who have resumed their Specie payments should immediately curtail their discounts," said Girard. He also suggested that such banks pay specie for all notes under five dollars at first and thus bring specie into gradual circulation. "I sincerely hope that you will obtain a compleat Law to prevent the exportation of Specie as far as practicable," he added. "I was against that commercial prohibition but now consider it indispensable [*sic*]." He suggested that gold for the far eastern trade be obtained by utilizing roundabout routing of vessels to Europe and then Asia. In this fashion, he pointed out, his own ships had imported more gold than they had exported. In closing, Girard observed that the government might incorporate a national bank. Such an institution would "prove very successful provided government is at least entrusted of one third the capital which would not be less than fifty million and that he should have the right to nominate directors. . . . A bank founded on that plan," said Girard, "would afford great resources to the United States, consolidate its credit and the operations of that Institution would promote the real interest of all prudent State Banks." Girard and Dallas clearly shared the belief that voluntarism would not accomplish a return to stable monetary conditions and that some agency of the government was needed to aid in the process. As the secretary lamented, "The charter restrictions of some of the banks . . . and the duty which the directors conceive they owe their constituents upon points of security and emolument interpose an insuperable obstacle for the establishment of a national medium through the agency of the State banks."[29]

The repeated failure to develop a national plan for the resumption of specie payments had a decided impact on all banks, including Girard's. The Philadelphia banks had been operating without a formal agreement since the suspension of specie payments in the preceding September. During that interval Girard pursued a policy of tentative expansion. As table 3 indicates, between the first and third quarters of 1815 total loans increased by 88 percent, bank notes in circulation by 99 percent, and individual deposits by 46 percent.

However, from the first of the year to 1 October 1815, Girard's holdings of unredeemable bank notes grew by nearly 67 percent. As holdings of such bank notes grew at all city banks, some systematic way to deal with the problem was needed. On 10 November 1815 the chartered institutions of Philadelphia reached an agreement. The main provisions of this pact were that (1) debtor banks should pay interest on balances above $25,000 until the balance should fall below $25,000; (2) debtor banks could pay by drawing on any other Philadelphia bank which was party to the agreement or with United States funded debt at 2 percent below its fair market value on the day of payment; (3) all participating banks were required to furnish information on their indebtedness on the first Monday of each month; (4) banks should not pay out the notes of other banks above ten dollars, but rather should return such notes to the issuing bank. The agreement was to take effect on the first Monday in December 1815.[30] This and similar agreements in New York and other cities were adopted out of necessity and did nothing to remedy the root causes of the monetary crisis. Girard, of course, was not a party to the arrangement but was wary of any agreement that united the banks of the city.

At the national level, Madison's annual message to Congress and Dallas' annual report on the Treasury expressed support for a national bank. Calhoun, the chairman of the Committee on a National Currency, requested Dallas' views on the problems of the currency. His reply contained the outline of a plan for a national bank, which envisioned a twenty-year charter and authorized capital of $35 million (35,000 shares at $100). The public was to purchase 280,000 shares and the government 70,000. Payment by the public was to consist of $7 million in specie and $21 million in funded United States debt. The president, with the advice and consent of the Senate, would appoint five of the bank's twenty-five directors. Notes of the bank, which was to be headquartered in Philadelphia, would not be legal tender but would be receivable for all governmental debts, and Congress (or in its absence the president) could authorize the suspension of specie payments.[31]

Calhoun had experienced a change of heart. Opposed to a bank which he felt was designed to relieve the financial exigency of the Treasury during wartime, he found a similar institution designed to restore monetary stability more palatable. On 8 January 1816, his committee reported a bill that closely paralleled Dallas' outline. Calhoun's bill moved through the House with surprising ease and very little change. Amendments to reduce the bank's capital, eliminate government ownership of bank stock, and prevent the president from appointing directors, were voted down easily. The Senate proved an equally easy hurdle, passing the bill with minor changes by a margin of 22 to 12 on 3 April. Agreement was reached between the legislative bodies on 5 April, and Madison signed the bill into law on 10 April 1816.

The immediate impact of the passage of the bank bill on Girard's bank and the chartered institutions was contractionary. Table 4 clearly

Table 4

Economic indicators following the adoption
of the national bank bill at Stephen Girard's Bank

Date		Total loans	Bank notes in circulation	Deposits (individual)	Loan/asset ratio
1816	1	$1,020,312	$252,357	$509,120	25.61
	2	805,392	198,502	524,595	20.12
	3	849,792	153,242	524,572	17.83
	4	730,280	128,192	466,616	15.13
1817	1	700,342	103,817	277,816	18.37
	2	700,860	104,182	217,021	20.82
	3	881,079	107,257	418,736	24.47
	4	1,026,257	112,260	379,376	27.58

Source: SGC, II, 393.

indicates a reduction of loans, bank notes in circulation, and individual deposits. This contraction was general among the banks of the city.

The reason for the contraction was not difficult to identify. A joint resolution of Congress, passed at the same time as the bank bill, required that after 20 February 1817 all payments to the United States be made in specie, Treasury notes, federal bank notes, or notes of specie-paying banks. If the new national bank went into operation on a specie-paying basis, as its charter required, before a general resumption, it would be quickly stripped of its gold and silver reserves. Moreover, if resumption was not attained by 20 February, the general public would have no way of legally collecting its debts. Given these conditions, resumption seemed imminent, and the banks reacted accordingly, reducing their liabilities in anticipation of specie demands. At Girard's bank the contraction appears to have been concentrated in the first quarter of 1817, with expansion the rule after that. As for the chartered banks, they resolved to take concerted action to reduce the number of bills discounted in anticipation of the resumption of specie payments. Although the participating institution failed to agree upon a uniform policy to achieve this goal, the Bank of North America and the Farmer's and Mechanic's Bank reduced accommodation paper, "warning their customers by circulars and announcing reductions by percentages."[32] Other banks simply refused to discount new commercial paper or severely restricted such activity.

Girard reported to Baring Brothers that he was importing gold, "being desirous to increase the specie which I have in the vaults of my Bank in view to be ready when some of our principal banks are disposed to resume their specie payments."³³ Efforts in this regard were somewhat successful, and the total specie holdings of the bank grew from $177,920.52 in April 1816 to $682,090.02 by October of the same year.

With the passage of the act incorporating the Second Bank of the United States, Dallas moved quickly to insure that Girard would play an influential role in formulating its policies. On 8 April 1816 in a letter marked "private and confidential," the secretary noted, "It is my intention to use your name as a Commissioner for receiving subscriptions to the National Bank." In addition Dallas noted that "the Government Directors must be appointed during the Spring: Tell me *in confidence,* whether you would prefer to be appointed here, or to be chosen by the stockholders."³⁴

"If I am appointed a Commissioner for receiving subscriptions to the National Bank," responded Girard, "I will endeavor to do my duty but as to be a Director of that Institution I am fearful that my commercial and other occupations will not permit me to accept the appointment." Not wishing to close any doors, however, Girard added, "should it be otherwise I would prefer to be nominated by the Government."³⁵ On 15 April, Dallas prodded Girard. "The nomination of directors of the National Bank must be made during the present session, and the Congress will probably adjourn on the 22nd instant. You must, therefore, tell me, by the return of the Mail, whether you consent to be named." By way of a caveat, Dallas observed that "By the Bank Act, it is declared that a Director of any other Bank, cannot be appointed a Director of the National Bank. If your establishment be regarded as a Bank, and you as a Director within the meaning of the Act, a difficulty may arise in the Senate, of which you should be apprised."³⁶ Girard gave his consent, and Madison signed his commission as a director of the Bank of the United States on 26 April 1816.

During the first week in May, the commissioners of the subscription to the BUS decided to open the books for that purpose on 4 July. By the terms of the bank's charter, subscriptions would be taken for twenty days, terminating on 23 July. Girard was determined to become a major stockholder of the BUS and to accomplish this end through the agency of his bank, which held the specie and government debt required for subscription and would also serve as the Philadelphia center for such subscription. Girard's position as commissioner for subscriptions in Philadelphia gave him a decided advantage in the competition for ownership of the new bank. The act of incorporation specified that it was lawful for any individual, company, or corporation to subscribe for any number of shares not exceeding three thousand. However, a subsequent provision stated that if the public's share of $28 million was not completely subscribed, "the subscriptions to complete the said sum shall be and remain open at Philadelphia . . . under the superintendance of the commissioners appointed for that place; and the subscriptions may be then made by any individual, company or corporation, for any number of shares, not exceeding in the whole amount required to complete the said sum of twenty-eight million dollars."[37] Should the public subscription fall short, those in a position to purchase stock in Philadelphia were free of the 3000-share limit.

The initial subscription required only 5 percent of the total purchase in specie, but nonetheless by 1 July gold dollars in Philadelphia were selling at 17 percent advance against bank notes.[38] On 4 July at 10 A.M., the subscription books were opened at Stephen Girard's Bank in Philadelphia and at other locations around the country. Girard immediately purchased the 3,000 shares allowed under the terms of the law, paying $15,000 in silver and the balance of $75,000 chiefly in 3 percent stock valued at 65.[39] Girard followed closely the subscription to the bank's stock at Philadelphia and elsewhere by means of his network of commercial intelligence. When the books closed on the twenty-third, it appeared probable that the public subscription would not be filled. The returns from New Orleans were the last to arrive, but more than a week before the official returns were received from that city, Girard indicated that the subscription there "will not exceed 3,000 shares." In that case, said Girard, "the subscription to the capital stock will be short about $3,000,000 which will be filled up with great rapidity."[40]

Plans were now quickly developed to take the remaining shares of the BUS. August 26 was set as the date for reopening the books. In the preceding week Girard held a series of meetings with William Jones and Pierce Butler, fellow directors of the BUS from Philadelphia.[41] During the interval it was decided that Girard would act as the spokesman for a syndicate to purchase all the unsold shares. Those who were not a party to the agreement would be frozen out. Receipts were issued to participants, such as the one issued to Astor: "For value received, I hereby promise to transfer to John Jacob Astor or order One Thousand Shares of the Bank of the United States, on which the first Instalment has been paid, as soon as the Books for that purpose shall be opened by the said Bank."[42] At the hour appointed for reopening the books, Girard stepped forward and subscribed to the remaining 29,736 shares, paying the first specie instalment of $148,680 and funded debt of $743,400.[43] Purchases of those involved in the syndicate ranged from Charles Graff's 50 shares to 5000 shares for J. W. McCullough of Baltimore.[44]

Of course Girard stood to profit from his acquisition of BUS stock.

The bank's holdings reached $532,585.55 in the third quarter of 1816, at which time BUS stock was already selling above par. In regard to the profits that stockholders in the BUS could expect, Girard predicted that "it will be immense and I am of opinion that if well conducted its solidity and credit will not be rivalled by any Bank in the world. . . ."[45] Girard admitted that "in subscribing largely I had two objects in view, the first was to promote the early operation of that indispensible [*sic*] institution and the 2nd to prevent the increase of a multiplicity of proxies which had already accumulated so as to give more votes to 31 shares than to those who owned upwards of 20,000." This reference to a proliferation of proxies had an ominous ring. The BUS charter specified that an individual might cast a maximum of thirty votes, regardless of the number of shares he owned. Thus someone who held thirty shares (representing an investment of $3,000) and one proxy vote might exert more influence than the owner of several thousand shares who had no proxies. Girard was determined that the leadership of the bank should reside in the business community or "the merchants of the U.S. who generally will compose ¾ of the Directors of the Bank and Offices of [Discount and Deposit]."[46] The responsibility for administering the BUS should be assumed in proportion to one's share of ownership. To Girard the natural leaders of the BUS were those who made its existence possible through large purchases of its capital stock.

Concomitant with the sale of BUS stock, Dallas attempted to prod the banks into gradual redemption along the lines suggested by Girard the previous October. In describing the abortive attempt, Girard noted that "the Secretary of the Treasury has in his polite way invited the Banks to pay Specie commencing with the 1st October next when all payments from 5 dollars and under are to be made in coin otherwise the notes of the banks which will not comply with that arrangement will not be received in payment of the Revenue." Girard added that "in consequence of that publication a quantity of public stock has been placed for sale in the hands of the brokers which has reduced its price to 95 percent."[47]

Such anxiety, however, was premature, for the major banks had no intention of being forced into resumption before they were ready. In early September, representatives of the larger institutions assembled in Philadelphia. Girard reported the results of the meeting to David Parish. "A committee appointed by the chartered Banks of New York, Philadelphia and Baltimore have met in this city where they have decided to resume their Specie payments on the first of July next."[48] The banks were unwilling to reduce loans further for fear of embarrassing their already strained customers.[49] Moreover, the wholesale liquidation of government stock would seriously depress the market. There was also the question of unanimity, and most bankers were convinced that unless all agreed to resumption it could not succeed. Finally, the BUS and its branches were not expected to be in full operation before July, and their assistance would be essential to successful resumption of specie payments.

The last rebuff was too much for Dallas. He officially resigned the post of secretary of the treasury on 20 October 1816 and was succeeded by William H. Crawford of Georgia.[50] The new secretary immediately confronted the problem of resumption, and on 20 December launched a concerted effort to achieve this goal. He pointed out that the BUS was slated to commence operations in January 1817 and that all public deposits would be transferred to that institution immediately. "If the determination of the banks to resume specie payments on the 1st of July, 1817 . . . is persevered in," said Crawford, "there will be no hesitation on ordering the transfer to be made with as little delay as the interest of the community will admit."[51] However, Crawford stated, should the banks agree to resume specie payments on 20 February 1817, "the public money now in their vaults shall not be transferred to those of the Bank of the United States, and that, between that day and the first of July next, as small a portion of that sum shall be drawn as the demands upon the Treasury will admit." Crawford added that "in deciding upon the question submitted to their consideration the friendly character and disposition of the Bank of the United States . . . ought not to be overlooked. The deep interest which the Treasury has in the support of bank credit, and the connexion which it has with the Bank of the United States would, independently of the known disposition of that institution to conciliate the State banks, be sufficient to protect them against an illiberal policy on its part." Crawford ended his communication by stating that "candor compels me to state there exists no reason to expect that the resolution of the last session of Congress, relative to the collection of the revenue after the 20th of February next will be rescinded."

The question of the disposition of Treasury funds was of some importance to Girard and his bank. As a depository for the Treasury, it held large sums of government revenue. In July the bank held $468,637.39 in its Treasury account, and by year's end this total had grown to $910,987.89.[52] On the latter date, Girard's bank also held $443,695.44 in the account of the commissioners of the Bank of the United States. In addition, Girard's vaults were bursting with some $682,090.08 in specie, which was largely related to the bank's connections with the Treasury and the BUS.

Crawford's proposal was not greeted enthusiastically by the banks, and Girard himself was noncommittal. He informed Crawford that it was his intention to resume specie payments "immediately after two of the oldest Banks of this City have adopted that desirable mode of resuming gradually their Specie payments. I hope that it will be convenient for the Pennsylvania, Farmer's and Mechanic's and North America Bank or two of them to do it on the 20th Feby next."[53] Unlike most of the chartered institutions, Girard was willing to consider a partial resumption.

The more responsible banks were now forced to conclude that a decision on resumption that satisfied their needs and those of the Treasury was needed, and needed quickly. Once more the bankers convened in Philadelphia on 24 and 25 January to set a date for the simultaneous resumption of specie payment. The representatives agreed on 20 February 1817, provided that a satisfactory arrangement could be worked out with Crawford and the BUS. On 31 January an agreement was reached between a committee of the convention of banks and the board of the BUS. The banks of New York, Philadelphia, Baltimore, Richmond, and Norfolk agreed to commence and continue specie payments "for all demands upon them, and reciprocally to support the credit of each other in their several districts, upon any emergency, until the balances between them are finally paid off."[54] The agreement to meet all demands in specie made the obligation of the banks acceptable in payment of federal taxes under conditions laid down by the joint resolution of Congress.

The terms offered by the Treasury and the BUS were generous. Government balances in depository banks were to be transferred to the BUS and "retained in its vaults until 1st July next when same shall be paid off with interest. . . ."[55] By assuming the state banks' liabilities to the Treasury, the BUS virtually lent the state banks sufficient funds to settle their obligations to the government and enabled them to pay the Treasury at once without seriously contracting their own obligations. Moreover, participating banks were permitted to pay debts to the BUS by drawing on deposits in other cooperating banks, thereby avoiding specie movements. As a final effort to soften the blow of resumption, the BUS would not demand balances due from the state banks until it had itself lent $2 million each in New York and Philadelphia, $1.5 million in Baltimore, and $500,000 in Virginia. In cases where local demand was insufficient to absorb this inflow of credit, the banks themselves would have the option of taking what remained. This procedure would ease the pressure on local money markets until the banks adjusted to the new system. In a nine-point plan officially adopted on 1 February 1817, the state banks and the BUS agreed to "interchange pledges of good faith and friendly offices," and in the event of an emergency to come to the aid of one another within reasonable limits.[56]

Girard reacted quickly to the decision of the state banks. He desired the same favored treatment as those institutions who were parties to the agreement but had not been included in their deliberations. In an attempt to influence Secretary Crawford, Girard informed him on 28 January of a reversal in his position. Referring to his refusal to respond in the affirmative to Crawford's circular of 20 December, he admitted that "since that period I have meditated on the expediency of paying specie for the Notes of my Bank although the results of my reflections presents [*sic*] many obstacles particularly if two or three banks of this city do not agree to redeem their obligations in a like manner, yet relying on your disposition to afford every reasonable facility to those money establishments whose conduct merits your confidence I have decided to pay Specie . . . and hope that you will give in time the necessary instructions so the public money deposited in my Bank shall be drawn in such a manner as not to derange its daily operations."[57]

However, Crawford reminded Girard that "the conditions upon which your acceptance was made to depend having failed, it was considered void, and an order was issued on the 24th ultimo to the Treasurer, directing him to take the necessary measures to transfer the public deposits in the Banks of Pennsylvania, Delaware and Maryland, to the Bank of the United States."[58] Crawford emphatically added that "the benefits resulting from the general and unreserved execution of that measure are too important to the community to suffer the interest of any State bank . . . to interfere with it." Finally, noted Crawford, "considering the advantage which the banks which heretofore had the public deposits have derived from them, there cannot be any reasonable doubt of their ready acquiescence in a measure to which the other State banks have acceded with alacrity." Girard's request for special consideration had politely but firmly been denied.

The BUS commenced limited operations in January 1817, and 20 February brought resumption of specie payments by the major banks. On 13 February, Girard indicated to John Stoney of Charleston that he would pay specie for his notes, but "in regard to deposits they shall be paid in notes of the Banks of the city which can easily be converted into solid metal if those banks pay specie for them the depositors will be furnished with bank notes which can be converted into specie."[59] Girard's supply of gold and silver were to be protected at the expense of the specie reserves of other city banks. His refusal to pay specie for deposits, however, was in conflict with the plan adopted by the other banks. Thus when Girard attempted to deposit his Treasury funds on 19 February, he was refused the privilege of making the delayed transfer to the BUS on the basis of noncompliance with the general agreement. It was decided to grant his bank the privileges of the association if he would accept the terms agreed upon. Anxious to make the best settlement possible, Girard reluctantly agreed and arranged for the payment of a draft on Stephen Girard's Bank to the BUS in favor of the Treasury. On 26 February 1817, $884,119.43 was transferred to the BUS. The same day Girard reported to Crawford that "on the 20th present month my Bank commenced and has continued to pay Specie for her notes and paid deposit in notes of the Banks of this city until this day when she has resumed her species payments, agreeably to the proposal and agreement before mentioned."[60] To his old friend Caesar Rodney of Wilmington, Girard remained adamant. "I am still of the opinion," he wrote, "that I was not one of the parties yet being desirous to cultivate a good understanding with the Bank of the United States on the 25th inst. I have accepted the proposal and the operations of my Bank are conducted in conformity."[61]

Girard's close relationship with the Treasury was now nearly at an end. Treasury deposits, which had exceeded $900,000.00 in January, fell to $5,737.78 in April, and an additional $443,695.44 was paid into the BUS in February on behalf of the commissioners of the subscription to the Bank of the United States. Table 5 attests to the impact of these transactions.

Table 5

Economic indicators following the resumption of
specie payments at Stephen Girard's Bank

Date		Loans	Specie	Bank notes	Deposits	Loan/asset ratio
1817	1	$ 700,342	$177,730	$898,140	$277,815	18.37
	2	700,860	179,195	813,009	217,021	20.82
	3	881,079	327,721	807,183	418,736	24.47
	4	1,026,257	371,013	799,842	379,376	27.58
1818	1	1,035,104	275,233	687,791	319,955	29.74
	2	1,066,154	220,567	819,177	200,608	30.24
	3	1,285,089	220,253	759,375	373,711	34.08
	4	1,269,221	328,443	752,249	289,728	37.27
1819	1	1,351,150	363,880	635,466	320,992	36.76
	2	1,365,487	472,864	648,730	432,572	36.95
	3	1,092,066	625,741	694,832	414,420	29.43
	4	1,047,885	566,050	695,288	254,540	29.01

Source: SGC, II, 393 and 147–50.

Of great concern was the bank's inability to quickly expand loans and discounts following resumption. As Girard himself was quick to note, the arrangement between the BUS and the convention of state banks "to pay specie and in case of a run to support each other until the 1st July next" made it necessary to "curtail my discounts and to reserve all my resources to comply in case of need with the agreement forementioned."[62] After the 1 July deadline, loans and discounts expanded rapidly toward presuspension levels.

Likewise, the specie reserves of the bank increased substantially after July 1817 but also showed some improvement over the first half of the year. Any apprehension that Girard felt over raids on his specie supplies quickly dissipated following resumption. He cheerfully indicated to Stoney in Charleston that the demand for specie "may be said to be nominal owing to the confidence and friendly disposition of those who had funds in said Banks or hold the notes thereof."[63] Things went smoothly during the first week after resumption, and Girard noted that "from the moment when my Bank was opened on the 20th cur't. until 3 o'clock this afternoon application for Specie which was made to my Bank has been principally for her notes and . . . all the solid metal which has been paid out between those two periods is about $6,000." Concerning the agreement he had so reluctantly embraced, Girard noted in March that "it requires each of us to exchange our notes and to pay or receive the balance in entering it in our Bank Book."[64] In addition he observed that "in regard to our Specie payments for all demands . . . we met with no difficulties. . . ." On another occasion he boasted that "the daily operations of my bank present a more favorable prospect than what I had reason to expect," and added that since resumption his supply of gold and silver was gradually increasing.[65]

The bank's holdings of notes from other institutions slowly diminished after resumption. From a high point of $1,184,802.60 in October 1816, such holdings shrank to $687,791.00 in the first quarter of 1818. The return to more normal conditions also prompted an increase in the loan/asset ratio, which attained presuspension levels by the second quarter of 1818.

In sharp contrast to Girard's success in achieving a smooth resumption of specie payments were his dealings with the BUS. The first elections of directors by the stockholders occurred on 28 October 1816 and were a severe disappointment to Girard. In his view, "intrigue and corruption had framed a ticket for twenty directors of the Bank of the United States who . . . appear to have been elected for the purpose of securing the presidency to Wm. Jones, the cashier's office to Jonathan A. Smith and for other pecuniary views."[66]

Table 6

Distribution of shares and authorized votes,
Bank of the United States

City	Number of shares	Names in which taken	Shares per name	Votes authorized	Votes authorized/ shares taken (4)/(1)
Boston	24,023	364	65.99	4,355	.181
New York	20,012	2,641	7.57	6,450	.322
Philadelphia	88,520	3,566	24.82	19,260	.217
Baltimore	40,141	15,628	2.56	22,187	.522

Source: Ralph C. H. Catterall, *The Second Bank of the United States* (Chicago, 1903) p. 39, n. 2.

The issue of proxies, which had prompted Girard to complete the BUS subscription in August, had now become critical. As table 6 indicates, the distribution of shares and the distribution of authorized votes differed greatly. Philadelphia accounted for more shares than Boston, New York, and Baltimore combined and over twice the shares distributed in Baltimore alone. Yet the latter city was credited with more authorized votes than Philadelphia. The explanation, of course, lies in the number of subscribers and the limit of thirty votes per shareholder contained in the bank's charter. In Baltimore, large blocks of stock were subscribed to for long lists of buyers (often fictitious), who then immediately gave their proxy to an agreed-upon individual. By this process, each share taken in Baltimore produced over one-half of an authorized vote, and each taken in Philadelphia, less than one-fourth of one. At first Girard attempted to lead a stockholders' revolt, calling on the southern share-owners to provide him with enough proxies to oust the Jones clique from office. Failing in this endeavor, Girard decided to reduce his bank's holdings of BUS stock, which by November was selling at $43 for $30 paid in.[67]

Soon after the BUS began operations, Girard found himself at odds with its administration. Anticipating the philosophy of Biddle, Girard favored an arrangement under which the BUS in Philadelphia would issue all notes and furnish these to the various branches. Such notes would be redeemable only in Philadelphia, and the system would provide for a uniform currency as well as centralized control. However, the plan adopted was to have each branch raise its own capital and issue its own notes, payable at any other branch, including Philadelphia. The question as Girard saw it was whether "the Bank of the U.S. is to be the National

Bank of the Union or placed on like footing as a common State Bank . . . as it respects the circulation of Bank Notes."[68] Girard remained determined to topple Jones from the presidency of the BUS. "If I live twelve months longer," he vowed, "I intend to use my means, activity and influence to change and replace the majority of the present directors by honest and independent men. . . ."[69]

In July 1817, the BUS declared a semiannual dividend of 2.6 percent. This pleased the stockholders and solidified support for Jones, but the profits thus distributed had been achieved by a rapid and often indiscriminate expansion of loans. This only served to strengthen Girard's misgivings about the bank's leadership, but he now began to view his struggle against the Jones faction as futile. On 31 December 1817, he wrote to John Quincy Adams, the secretary of state, "Although I am much flattered by the honor which the President of the United States has . . . conferred on me by appointing me one of the Directors of the Bank of the United States . . . yet owing to the increase of my private Business *and other circumstances* I am under the necessity to resign."[70]

By July 1818 the BUS was in serious trouble. The rapid expansion of loans by the western and southern branches flooded the country with branch notes, which normal patterns of trade deposited in the northern and eastern branches for redemption. In an effort to stem the tide, the directors ordered curtailment of discounts. On 28 August 1818, branch offices were directed to receive for payment in specie only their own notes, except as payment for government obligations.[71] This was a serious blow to the acceptability of BUS notes and made the BUS branches indistinguishable in practice from the state banks. Rumors were now abroad that "some leaders of the Bank of the U.S." were involved in the manipulation of the institution's stock. Girard was pessimistic and felt "that owing to the improper management of the Interest of that institution her stock is on a rapid decline which I can assure you hurts my feelings, particularly when I take into view that I have contributed towards obtaining the charter of that Bank more than any living man in Pennsylvania."[72]

By late October, a group of South Carolina stockholders was ready to challenge the bank's management. In Girard's opinion a change in management was overdue but could probably not be achieved until the election of 1820.[73] However, on 25 November Representative John C. Spencer of New York called for "a committee to be appointed to inspect the books and examine into the proceedings of the Bank of the United States, and to report whether the provisions of its charter have been violated or not."[74] The committee, with Spencer as chairman, was approved on 30 November and began its investigation.

While the activities of the directors could scarcely stand close scrutiny, the selection of the bank's officers was at hand, and it was unlikely that the committee's report would be completed in time to affect the outcome. Jones won re-election easily but was opposed by a group of South Carolinians and others, including Girard. This group succeeded in procuring a seat on the board of directors for Langdon Cheves of South Carolina. These events instilled new hope in Girard with respect to the BUS and influenced a potentially important portfolio change in his bank. He wrote to Baring Brothers that "many stock speculators will be ruined by their wild ideas of making at once considerable fortune. As soon as the majority of the stock of that Bank is placed in the hands of Capitalists competent directors will be appointed and public confidence will revive. I have still on hand a few thousand shares which cost me par and on which all the instalments are paid. I intend to keep them and run my chances particularly as I am confident that on the first Monday of January, 1820 a total change will take place."[75]

Girard now urged the dissidents to apply to Congress for a change in the charter "so every stockholder who is a citizen and resides in the U.S. be entitled to one vote for each share which he has in that Bank. . . ."[76] As a precedent Girard cited the government's appointment of five directors based on its one-fifth share of the bank's equity. Such a change would have left Girard with 4,500 votes on his own account, plus the support of the anti-Jones faction. Should Congress refuse to act on such a petition, said Girard, "the money stockholders will have no other alternative but to divide their shares at an early period and to fight their enemy with equal weapons."

The Spencer Committee's report was made public on 16 January 1819. It found President Jones and other directors guilty of violating the charter of the BUS. Speculation in government stock, illegal stock-loan procedures, illegal payment of dividends, and the willful proliferation of proxies were among the charges leveled. The committee recommended no specific action, feeling that the existing law and executive action could remedy the situation. On 21 January *Binn's Evening Paper* noted, "We stop the press to announce that Wm. Jones Esq. has resigned the office of President of the United States Bank."[77] Girard was now hopeful of Cheves' election, confiding to Stoney that "should Mr. Landgdon Cheves . . . arrive shortly it is probable that the former will be elected President."[78] By 26 January BUS shares began to rise in price, a reaction to the anticipated change in the bank's management. At month's end the government announced its nominees for director, including three from Philadelphia—John Connelly, John Steele, collector of the port, and Nicholas Biddle, attorney at law. Girard noted with some satisfaction that "the character of those gentlemen stand [*sic*] with us very high. . . ."[79]

Cheves arrived in Philadelphia on 2 March 1819 and met with Girard that same forenoon. Girard was satisfied that Cheves would answer the stockholders' expectations in every respect and, with Cheves' friends, prevailed on the South Carolinian to seek the presidency of the bank. Even though it was well known that Monroe had selected him for nomination to the Supreme Court, Cheves agreed. The man who, as Speaker of the House of Representatives, had cast the decisive vote against Dallas' bank bill in 1814 was now the champion of the probank Republicans. Cheves was elected President of the BUS on 6 March 1819.

The day following Cheves' election, the Supreme Court, in the case of *McCulloch* v. *Maryland,* unequivocally established the right of the BUS to establish offices of discount and deposit in the various states and declared such branches free from state taxation. The change in the bank's management and the favorable decision of the Court gave rise to a steady increase in the price of BUS stock, and Girard increased his bank's holdings in 1822, 1823, and 1824, reaching $726,725.12 by the fourth quarter of 1824. The dividends received in the bank from BUS stock rose from a low of $7,350.00 in 1821 to $27,980.00 by 1824, and continued to increase until Girard's death in 1831. The total holdings never fell below 10 percent of the bank's earning assets.[80]

Girard's interest in the management of the BUS waned following the election of Cheves to the presidency. His dealings with the BUS were reduced to the routine of adjusting his bank's portfolio holdings of BUS stock and day-to-day relations with the BUS itself. As the largest bank in Philadelphia, the BUS affected the accounts of all city institutions. The net balances of Stephen Girard's Bank with the BUS were generally positive before 1824 and negative after that date. The BUS policy of controlling the issue of state banks, which was instituted by Biddle in 1823, may account for the consistent claims that that institution held against Girard's assets. To make such a control policy credible, the BUS was forced to maintain net positive balances with the state banks in question. Thus when presented with their notes for redemption, banks could not simply write off the value of such notes from accounts at the BUS.

Similarly, during the 1820s, Girard's relations with the Treasury deteriorated. During 1814 and 1815, Dallas repeatedly appealed to Girard for short-term loans to enable the Treasury to pay its bills. Repeatedly, Girard refused to make such advances. Neither did he take much interest in the long-term issues of 1815, 1821, and 1824. Treasury debt was decreasing, and the bank's interests increasingly focused on the private capital markets. Thus 1817 marked the end of Girard's close association with the Treasury, and 1819 the end of his special interest in the BUS. The last twelve years of the Girard Bank's existence were characterized by a close relationship with the chartered institutions of Philadelphia and a less independent course of action. One of the consequences of the bank's acceptance on an equal footing by both the government and the city's banking community was a certain loss of the independence and freedom of action that had characterized the early years of its existence. During the 1820s Stephen Girard's Bank became indistinguishable from its chartered, incorporated competitors.

5

Competition and Cooperation

Girard's relations with the Treasury and the Bank of the United States had their parallel in the private sector. Indeed, the difficulties encountered by Stephen Girard's Bank in gaining acceptance within the Philadelphia financial structure reveal much about the competition and cooperation that characterized early nineteenth-century banking. Moreover, the question of Girard's status was clouded by the fact that his institution was unique in many respects. Despite his enormous wealth and power within the commercial community, the success of Stephen Girard's Bank was in no way insured.

By the spring of 1812, the name of Stephen Girard was a familiar one in the major commercial centers of Europe and America. In London, Amsterdam, Hamburg, Copenhagen, Riga, Saint Petersburg and other cities, it was common practice for successful merchants to pursue limited banking functions. Thus among Girard's acquaintances in the business world, there was little surprise at his decision to initiate a private banking house. It soon became evident, however, that Stephen Girard's bank would differ in both scale and function from its European and American counterparts. Girard's institution was to be a bank of deposit and issue, in contrast to the European merchant banking houses, which carefully eschewed issuing bank-note liabilities. In short, it represented something new on the American banking scene.

In his new role as banker, Girard faced the prospect of establishing new relationships and lines of communication within the tightly controlled financial community. Ironically, the notoriety he had achieved in mercantile circles and the prestige associated with his takeover of the late Bank of the United States proved to be a handicap in establishing ties with the other Philadelphia institutions. Opposition to new banks in early America was quite often a local affair. In the first place, the scarcity of gold and silver prompted many banks to view competitors as rivals for specie reserves as well as profits, and as soon as each entered the field it in turn opposed the entry of others.[1] Second, the parochial character of the nation's capital markets and its banking system made new local institutions appear to be interlopers, while new banks in other commercial centers were often welcomed as useful correspondents. Thus the lack of interregional capital markets protected local institutions from outside competition but restricted their own lending activities to the extent that they were hard pressed to preserve what monopoly power they possessed.

Girard's bank was not the first to encounter opposition in Philadelphia. The Philadelphia Bank, for example, began operations as an unincorporated institution in September 1803, at which time the other banks of the city refused to accept its notes. In retaliation, the cashier of the Philadelphia Bank was ordered to present the notes of all other city banks to the issuing institutions for payment in specie. Despite this pressure on their specie supply, the chartered banks did not relent, and when the Philadelphia Bank decided to seek a state charter, the other banks of the city voiced strenuous opposition. As part of this opposition, the Bank of Pennsylvania went so far as to offer favors to the state in return for a monopoly charter, claiming that the state's share of ownership in the Bank of Pennsylvania would decrease in value if new banks were chartered. Failing in this effort, the Bank of Pennsylvania offered the state a bribe of $200,000 in an effort to block the charter of the Philadelphia Bank. When the latter institution was finally chartered on 5 March 1804, it was required to give the state a "gratuity" of $135,000 and to accept from the state at par $300,000 in 6 percent United States stock in return for a like amount of the bank's capital stock, even though the bonds were selling at a discount.[2] In addition, the state retained the option to purchase additional shares of stock, the right to appoint six of the bank's twenty-two directors, and the option to borrow $100,000 from the bank for ten years at 5 percent.[3] The size of the payments offered to prevent or obtain the granting of a banking charter and the eagerness with which they were paid are some measure of the degree of monopoly power that both established banks and prospective banks could wield.

The Philadelphia Bank marked its acceptance into the banking community by appointing a committee to "cooperate" with similar committees of the other institutions. In a few years, these committees became known collectively as the "General Committee," and met to discuss and settle issues of common interest to the city's banks. It was not unusual for the policies of the major banks in a commercial center such as Philadelphia to be arrived at jointly.[4] During the early years of its existence the General Committee's deliberations were likely to be of a constructive nature and dealt with such problems as clearing operations, overdrafts, and other areas that affected the efficiency of the city's banking system. The committee even led a campaign to recharter the BUS. However, as time went on, the nature of this cooperation began to change and tended either to brake down altogether or to degenerate into a collusive opposition to prospective entrants.

Stephen Girard's Bank appeared on the scene during an unsettled era in Philadelphia banking. There and elsewhere new banks were appearing to service the credit needs of those neglected by the older, established institutions, and some of the most important barriers to entry for new institutions were already crumbling. Although bank profits were high by contemporary standards it was nonetheless dissatisfaction with the loan policies of the existing institutions that played the major role in encouraging the formation of rival banks.[5] The new banks were characterized by a new and different kind of leadership as well as a different clientele. The directors were likely to be small-business men such as shopkeepers or mechanics, and, what was even more shocking to the established banks, they were often Republicans.[6] If unable to obtain a charter, these new banks often operated as "limited partnerships" or "limited companies." Such hybrid forms of business organization offered the relative safety of limited liability without the official blessing of the state legislature. These unauthorized institutions were not bound by the provisions of a charter, nor were they effectively controlled by the states' laws dealing with banking.

When the radical Republicans gained control of the Pennsylvania legislature, a new approach to the question of banking came to prevail. The lawmakers of the commonwealth favored the expansion of banks, particularly in the western, rural regions of the state, but recognized the need to exert legislative and statutory control over the institutions so authorized. Thus the general thrust of legislative activity dealing with banks during the first fifteen years of the nineteenth century was aimed at eliminating the unchartered and unregulated institutions and replacing them with a large number of incorporated banks. While the unchartered banks found themselves the target of legislative proposals, the chartering of the Farmer's and Mechanic's Bank of Philadelphia by the Act of 16 March 1809 heralded the coming of a decade of unlimited increase in the number of Pennsylvania banks.[7] Thus the established institutions of Philadelphia faced increased chartered competition at the same time as Girard's large private house commenced operations. Under these circumstances it is not surprising that the city institutions refused to receive Girard's notes on deposit, established no mutual accounts for clearing purposes, and, in general, disapproved of his activities.

Moreover, Girard did not fit neatly into the structure of joint committees and interlocking directorates which the older banks utilized to control competition. He was by reputation a loner, and a Republican one at that. Girard was also an entrepreneur in the truest sense of the word. This was in marked contrast to the other banks of the city, where the entrepreneur, that is, the actual leader of the enterprise, could be found among the bank presidents only in exceptional cases. In these institutions, dilution of leadership was the rule. The day-to-day operations were under the direction of the cashier, and it was that group that became the first professional bankers in the country and the progenitors of the modern banking profession.[8] In the latter regard, Girard was indeed fortunate, for he had acquired the services of George Simpson, formerly the cashier of the BUS. In all respects Stephen Girard's Bank was an establishment to be reckoned with, and the apprehension of the city's chartered banks was evident and justified.

Undeterred by the opposition of the Philadelphia banks, Girard commenced operations and quickly moved to establish working relationships with other institutions. As a first step in this direction, Jonathan Smith, the cashier of the Bank of Pennsylvania, presented to Girard on 10 May 1812 "a letter of credit on the Bank of Delaware at Wilmington for any amount you may want in cash from that Bank."[9] Having established his bank's ability to discount notes payable in Delaware, Girard looked to the deep South. He informed Christopher Fitzsimmons of Charleston, South Carolina, of his new venture and noted that during the course of the operations of his establishment, "I will have occasion to apply to one of your Banks, either for collecting Bills on my account or otherwise. I beg that you will inform me of the one whose conduct merits public confidence."[10] Fitzsimmon's reply was encouraging. "The oldest Bank here," he noted "is the Bank of South Carolina of which I have been a director for Seventeen years." He noted that "the Bank of South Carolina proposes to apply to the legislature of the State, at their meeting in November next to grant them liberty to deal in Bills of Exchange at their current discount," and added, "in case of that being granted of which there is little doubt, an advantageous Business may be done between this City and Philadelphia in the way of Exchange and it is likely that if the Bank of South Carolina gets the amendment to its Charter that they will make some proposition to you on that subject."[11] Girard subsequently did choose the Bank of South Carolina as his Charleston correspondent, and this initial contact was the beginning of a long and profitable relationship.

Closer to home, Girard had established a working relationship with the Mechanic's Bank of Baltimore by 2 June. On that day Simpson received from D. A. Smith, the cashier of the Mechanic's Bank, "Sundry Notes and Bills for collection on account of Stephen Girard Banker amounting to $68,112.78."[12] The first New York contact was with the Bank of New York on 4 June. Simpson sent that institution's cashier, Charles Wilkes, some $4,710.20 in bills for collection, "by direction of Mr. Stephen Girard who has commenced the Banking business in the house lately occupied by the Bank of the United States."[13] This relationship was not destined to be a permanent one, however, for on 5 September 1812 the newly chartered Bank of America contacted Girard concerning an account. In particular the Bank of America wanted a correspondent that would "keep but one account in New York."[14] Simpson also received an invitation from the Cashier of the newly established City Bank of New York, indicating that institution's desire to initiate a correspondent relationship with Stephen Girard's Bank.[15]

The strictly bilateral arrangement suggested by the Bank of America apparently was the most appealing, for on 17 September Simpson informed Jonathan Burrall, the cashier, that although Girard had about $18,000 in the Bank of New York, "in the future all bills, etc. will be forwarded to your Bank only."[16] The exclusive arrangement with the Bank of America was particularly important to Girard because the other Philadelphia banks refused his notes and presented them for payment in specie. As the sole Philadelphia correspondent of the Bank of America, Girard was able to reduce the volume of notes that fell into the hands of his rivals. Notes of the Girard bank which made their way to New York would be redeemed at the Bank of America by reciprocal agreement and then returned to Girard, at which time the Bank of America's account would be credited by the appropriate amount. For this very reason, Girard appeared to favor such bilateral correspondent relationships whenever and wherever they could be arranged.

To complete his eastern network, Girard approached the Massachusetts Bank of Boston. "It is the intention of Mr. Girard," wrote Simpson to James Thwing, cashier, "to transmit to your Bank such . . . bills and notes payable in Boston as may from time to time be lodged for collection." In return, Girard would expect to receive from the Massachusetts Bank "those you may have occasion to collect in this city."[17] The Massachusetts Bank had already corresponded with the Bank of

North America in Philadelphia but informed Simpson that if the Directors "think of dividing the business in your city," he would be informed.[18] Evidently the management of the Massachusetts Bank decided in favor of Girard, and on 1 January 1813 the bank's balance sheet indicated a net credit of $250 at that institution.

Girard was now in a position to discount and collect notes payable in all the major commercial centers on the Atlantic seaboard. However, much of Philadelphia's trade, particularly that in agricultural commodities such as grain, flour, and meat products, was a product of its rich and varied hinterland. To finance this inland trade, Girard needed correspondents in major interior cities such as Lancaster and Reading. Soon after commencing operations, Girard moved to secure a western correspondent. On 8 June 1812 Simpson informed Samuel Clendenin, cashier of the Farmer's Bank of Lancaster, "I have the pleasure to inform you that Mr. G. is willing to receive your bank notes in payments and also pay drafts for Such Sums as you may deposit in his Banking House and exchange Notes of his Bank which you may receive from time to time as may be hereafter arranged.[19] To open their account, the Farmer's Bank was prepared to send some $150,000 in Philadelphia bank notes to Simpson for collection and credit to their account. Clendenin was also curious as to whether Girard could or would receive from them as deposits the notes of banks in adjoining states, and if so, which ones.[20] Simpson appeared pleased with the suggested arrangement and replied, "This Bank will receive for collection such bills and notes as may be payable in this city and pass the same to credit of your Bank when paid—The notes of Bank of New York . . . and Mechanic's Bank of Baltimore . . . will be received as a deposit and placed to your credit but we have not yet made arrangements with other distant Banks when any shall be made, I will give you notice, and will be always happy to render any accommodations in our power."[21] Of particular interest to the Farmer's Bank, which, like so many inland institutions, suffered from an eastward drain of specie, was Girard's offer that "for any of the Notes of the Bank in this City or any sums to your credit" we will "pay the amount in specie if more convenient to your institution."[22] This arrangement was quite favorable to the Farmer's Bank, since it assured that their notes, receivable on deposit at Girard's bank, would now circulate at par in Philadelphia.[23] This system of insuring the circulation of country bank notes at par in Philadelphia was the precursor of a similar arrangement developed by the Suffolk Bank of Boston in 1819.

Girard's major foreign correspondent was the merchant banking house of Baring Brothers in London. The Barings had been Girard's chief intermediaries in his efforts to retrieve funds from the Continent before the War of 1812, and Alexander Baring accorded Girard a line of credit of £50,000 sterling with no security required. Other banks with which Girard established relations during the first two years of operation were the State Bank at Camden, the Bank of Columbia, the Bank of Washington, the Trenton Banking Company, the Merchant's Bank of New York, the City Bank of Baltimore, the Farmer's Bank at Reading, and the State Bank of Charleston.[24]

It is clear from the correspondence between Girard and Simpson and other institutions that the mutual accounts established were designed to facilitate interbank transactions and thus can be described as true banker's balances. Moreover, since Girard refused to pay interest on deposits of individuals or institutions, the accounts established by other institutions must have been set up to facilitate bank clearing operations. Table 7 indicates the size and relative importance of banker's balances at Stephen Girard's Bank betwen 1813 and 1831.

Table 7

Interbank deposits at
Stephen Girard's Bank, 1813–1831

Date (1 January)	Due from other banks	Due to other banks
1813	$ 34,085.48	$115,125.58
1814	52,173.00	499,398.00
1815	112,685.00	9,110.00
1816	25,286.24	133,041.08
1817	204,000.00	183,053.80
1818	15,148.59	231,478.92
1819	156,194.60	163,494.99
1820	143,428.73	149,448.10
1821	206,535.64	183,796.11
1822	358,145.87	198,370.58
1823	38,517.26	64,706.18
1824	65,477.53	129,386.81
1825	42,694.52	248,983.76
1826	51,306.37	89,564.07
1827	39,542.86	105,505.78
1828	34,554.72	332,358.53
1829	30,005.15	83,902.77
1830	29,105.15	92,929.59
1831	26,457.89	389,477.49
Average	$ 87,649.69	$179,112.17

Source: SGC, II, 393–94 and SGC, III, 101.

Deposits by other banks in Girard's bank generally exceeded Girard's deposits in other institutions, and this tendency was a natural outgrowth of Philadelphia's position as a commercial and financial center. The heavy inflow of bills payable in the city resulted in the crediting of the accounts of noncity banks. Deposits due other banks also increased when Girard received bank notes from these institutions on deposit. Periodically, as the bank's holdings of such notes reached a certain level, they would be exchanged with the issuing banks for Girard's notes, specie, or deposits according to an agreed-upon procedure. Girard and Simpson were very selective with regard to notes received for deposit, and with few exceptions only the notes of Philadelphia banks enjoyed this status.[25]

An accumulation of notes of a particular institution received special attention, and in some cases additional notes from that institution might be refused until adjustments were made. In May 1815, for example, Simpson informed Edward Worrell, cashier of the Bank of Delaware, that Mr. Girard "has directed me to discontinue for the present receiving the Notes of your Bank of which we have on hand above $5,000."[26] Simpson added the hope that "the course of Trade will shortly enable all the Banks in Delaware to provide for their notes which are daily offered on deposit by our customers the rejection is attended with some inconvenience." This was an important cause for concern by the Bank of Delaware, for if nonacceptance of its notes became widespread they would inevitably depreciate in value in the Philadelphia area. In this case, circumstances had changed sufficiently by 3 February 1816 to enable Simpson to inform Worrell that "we shall receive your notes on deposit from our customers as formerly," adding that "Mr. Girard is not willing to limit the Amount he will receive of your Bank notes, but must be governed by circumstances and the probability of your remittances."

The problems associated with the settlement of mutual obligations could most often be solved with the cooperation and understanding of correspondent banks, but problems involving specie often placed a great strain on the mutual good will of institutions. Specie raids could be engineered by banks themselves as Girard discovered in the aftermath of his participation in the loan of 1813, but such incidents were relatively rare. In most instances difficulties involving specie were the result of forces or events external to the banking system and quite beyond its control. Moreover, the decentralized structure of the nineteenth-century banking system contributed to the severity of these intermittent shortages of specie, turning each into a liquidity crisis. Consequently, problems associated with specie reserves and specie payments appear again and again in Simpson's bank correspondence with other cashiers.

In some cases it was a lack of confidence by the bank's own depositors or noteholders that placed a strain on the bank's specie supply. Samuel Clendenin of the Farmer's Bank of Lancaster described such an instance in September 1812. "We will call upon you about the beginning of next month for a small recruit of Silver or Specie," he told Simpson. "The sound of War has made our Germans very suspicious of paper currency; hence in the Country a continued exchange of other notes for ours, and a steady run upon us for Specie. We have nearly reestablished their confidence in Bank paper by counting out the dollars to them without hesitation." However, noted Clendenin, "this practice has cost us a vast quantity of Specie, and at the same time has thrown large sums of foreign notes into our hands."[27]

Such runs were not always inspired by fear or apprehension on the part of the bank's customers, however, as evidenced by Clendenin's letter of 5 October 1812. In it he requested between $20,000 and $30,000 in Pennsylvania notes because the clerk of the office of discount and deposit "in this place has this day returned from an excursion among the different Banks of Philadelphia, New York, Jersey, Delaware and Maryland and has collected about forty thousand dollars of our paper; with which, and all they could collect at this place and at Harrisburg, they have made a run upon us. They exceed us in their paper about fifteen thousand dollars and have drawn the Specie for the balance. I offered them a draft upon Mr. Girard, [but] this they refused replying that they felt no disposition to accommodate us."[28] The office of discount and deposit referred to was the Lancaster branch of the Bank of Pennsylvania. Had the branch accepted the draft on Girard it would have given the Bank of Pennsylvania a claim of $15,000, payable in specie at Stephen Girard's Bank. Under these circumstances, Girard was only too willing to come to Clendenin's rescue, and he promptly sent $65,000 in specie and $76,910 in notes to the beleaguered cashier.[29]

Runs and raids were not the sole causes of undue pressure on the available supply of gold and silver. As new banking institutions arose, many of them in the West, an increasing pressure was exerted on the specie supply and the stock of bank notes that were acceptable for deposit. In the spring of 1814, for example, Clendenin was late in remitting Philadelphia bank notes in exchange for those of the Farmer's Bank. He listed the principal causes for this tardiness as, first "the want of promptness in the Western Banks in making their payments to us," and second "the number of new banks which have arisen in our neighborhood whose Capital was made up principally of our paper. For this paper," said Clendenin, "we had to exchange the paper of the city Banks we should have sent to you."[30] By countenancing this delay, Girard was providing reserves for several of the newly established western banks at a time when specie was becoming increasingly difficult to obtain.

As the war with Britain dragged on into 1814, the banks of the Middle Atlantic states were placed under considerable pressure. Encouraged to expand bank notes and demand deposits in exchange for government bonds, the institutions of New York, Philadelphia, and Baltimore found their specie reserves dwindling in proportion to demand liabilities. Between 1814 and 1815, the chartered banks of Philadelphia alone increased bank notes in circulation from $154,071 to $579,603, and deposits from $214,715 to $442,818.[31] The refusal of New England's banks to participate in financing the war effort simply exacerbated the situation, for when the Treasury drew on accounts in the mid-Atlantic cities to make payments in New England, the banks of the latter region acquired specie claims on the institutions of Philadelphia and other cities.

Forsaking the cooperative spirit which had characterized interbank transactions in more peaceful times, the New England banks (in particular those of Boston) called for payment in specie. By mid-year the flow of gold and silver to the east had become a torrent, threatening the existence of some banks which had overextended themselves in the preceding period. As the New York banks were called on for specie, they in turn attempted to draw upon their correspondents in other cities. A bizarre incident in January 1814 underscored the seriousness of the situation and the need for a more cooperative attitude on the part of all banks. The story is related in a letter to Simpson from Jonathan Burrall, cashier of the Bank of America. "A circumstance has taken place here," said Burrall, "which I apprehend may make it necessary for us to bring more specie from Philadelphia."[32] It seems that the New England banks had taken New York notes very freely until their accumulation compelled them to put an end to the practice. The New England Bank of Boston then sent a representative to get $160,000 in specie from New York, but before the currency could be transferred it was deposited in the Manhattan Bank. The collector, it sems, was a director of the latter institution. A story was circulating in Boston, continued Burrall, of a "stoppage of a Bank in this City," and New York notes were exchanging at a 4 percent discount. "I calculate that this stroke of the Collector," he concluded, "will create both alarm and resentment in Boston," and he estimated that some $1.5 million due in Boston from the banks of New York would be called for, at least in part.

The latter fear proved justified, for on 8 February 1814 he informed Simpson, "The Banks in Boston, either in consequence of the detention of their money by the Collector or with the view of embarrassing the government in obtaining loans, appear to have determined to draw in all the money due to them from the Banks in New York and Philadelphia."[33] The sums involved were impressive. The New England Bank was demanding $500,000, and the State Bank of Boston $600,000, of which $200,000 was in Philadelphia. Burrall noted that the Bank of America might be forced to draw on Girard for more cash. On 12 February the New Yorker warned Simpson that he would ask for no less than $150,000 in gold if that was convenient for Stephen Girard's Bank.[34] Of course it was not convenient, but Simpson nonetheless replied that the specie would be ready when the Bank of America was prepared to send for it and that Philadelphia notes would be acceptable in exchange. "I observe what you say respecting the stopping of the money for the New England Bank," said Simpson, "which will no doubt have an injurious effect on the Paper of all Banks circulating to the Eastward." Simpson was quick to add, however, that "very little of this Bank can appear, as our discounts have been conducted with the greatest caution being for some time apprehensive of the present scarcity of specie."[35]

In spite of the caution exercised by Girard and Simpson, the bank's supply of specie was nearly depleted in the opening months of 1814. On the first of the year, the vaults held $483,462.23 in gold and $412,849.18 in silver, or a total of $896,311.41 in specie. By 1 April the bank's holdings of gold had been reduced to $118,968.27 and silver supplies had fallen to $55,175.20, a total of $174,143.47.[36]

Of course the chain of specie demands did not end with Girard. The same day that Simpson indicated his willingness to ship specie to New York, he informed the Farmer's Bank of Lancaster that "Mr. G. desires me to mention that owing to the great press for Specie in New York and Boston it will be very desirable that you sho restraint drawing on this Bank till your bal⁰ is paid off, as we must expect the demand on us will be very considerable."[37]

In facing this problem, Girard could expect no help from the other Philadelphia banks. As Simpson confided to Burrall, "all the Banks in this City being unfriendly to this establishment—we are obliged to use the greatest precaution in our business, and as they would rejoice at an opportunity of drawing the Specie from us, we have constantly to retain a large amount of their paper and to restrain our discounts more than usual with other banks."[38] In an effort to increase his supply of Philadelphia bank notes, Girard had Simpson inform D. A. Smith of the Mechanic's Bank of Baltimore that he would soon receive a packet containing $22,022 in his bank's notes, in exchange for which Girard desired notes of banks in New York, Philadelphia, Wilmington, and Lancaster. "We wish to avoid drawing specie from any Bank," said Simpson, "but must be prepared to meet the demands on us which may arise from the pressure on the New York Banks."[39]

The spring of 1814 was punctuated with correspondence between Simpson and Burrall on the scarcity of specie and several large shipments of gold and silver from Philadelphia to New York.[40] From the tone of this correspondence it was clear that the voluntary cooperation that characterized the relations between many major banks was about to break down. If conditions did not soon change for the better, a general process of liquidation would result, with the real possibility of a full-scale financial panic.

Summer brought no respite from the incessant demand for specie, and time and again Girard was forced to draw on the city banks for specie by presenting them with their own notes for redemption. Fearing that to continue this practice might cause those banks to retaliate, Girard instructed Simpson to inform Burrall that "owing to the difficulty of obtaining Specie from the banks of this city [we] will be obliged in future to pay your drafts in notes of these Banks by which your messenger can collect the Specie. The propriety of this measure will appear evident," said Simpson, "if you consider the hostility attributed to this establishment for making such large demands on the other Banks."[41] To insure that this attempt to shift the burden of specie redemption from his own institution to the New York banks did not raise doubts concerning his own solvency, Girard had Simpson add a disclaimer. "Business is so regulated that we always have claims against them for much more than could be demanded from us—and have also sufficient in our vaults to meet the engagements of this establishment." This statement was no idle boast, as table 8 indicates.

Girard's combined holdings of specie and bank notes of Philadelphia institutions were at all times far in excess of his own notes in circulation.

Table 8

**Note and specie holdings of Stephen Girard's Bank,
1814–1815**

Date		Notes in circulation	Specie	Notes of city banks
1814	1	$ —	$174,143	$ 653,406
	2	191,870	215,650	630,552
	3	110,730	208,161	858,824
	4	232,485	251,988	797,494
1815	1	136,237	232,610	1,187,975
	2	151,302	173,339	1,141,073
	3	271,887	174,279	1,108,085
	4	323,100	176,489	1,019,254

Source: SGC, II, 393–94, 147–50.

Indeed, there was no time during 1814 when specie reserves did not exceed bank notes in circulation. Girard's reasons for not drawing specie from the city banks had little to do with his vulnerability to retaliation. Having acquired the enmity of the Philadelphia banks by his very existence, he was loath to increase this hostility by personally pursuing the very unpopular course of drawing down their specie reserves in a period of financial distress.

During the liquidity crisis of 1814, New York was merely a way station for specie on its eastward journey. On 8 July, Burrall lamented that "an opinion prevails among the Banks in Philadelphia that the New York banks have pretty large sums in Specie and therefore they endeavor to supply themselves from this city. This is a mistake. I doubt whether the Banks here have so much by 50 percent as the Banks in Philadelphia. It goes faster than it is brought. We have brought a million of dollars and have not as much as we had when we sent for the first sum."[42]

In this crisis the most striking weaknesses of the early nineteenth-century banking system were evident. In general, the banks lacked the flexibility to respond quickly and correctly to changing economic conditions. More specifically, the principal reserves of the banking system— gold and silver—were not subject to control by a central monetary authority. Instead, these reserves were held by the banks and the public in proportions that varied with public preference and in total amounts that were subject to movements in international trade. Moreover, the general scarcity of specie in relation to the needs of the economic system induced some banks to operate with very low ratios of specie to demand liability, and others to commence operations with little or no specie. With regard to the latter, the Girard correspondence alludes to some country banks which utilized the notes of specie-paying institutions as a form of primary reserve. While this practice, if widespread, increased the volume of credit relative to specie supplies, it also increased the instability of the banking system and its vulnerability to exogenous shocks. In a period of liquidation, notes held by such banks would clearly add to the redemption woes of the large city institutions. Perhaps most importantly, by expanding the network of correspondent relationships, the banks had simplified the process of making payments over long distances but at the same time increased the interdependence of the banking system. The latter development made it more likely that the actions of a few major institutions in one city or region would quickly be felt throughout the country.

Thus the demand of the New England banks for specie left the institutions of Philadelphia, New York, and elsewhere with few choices. They could sell earning assets, such as government stock, to obtain the needed specie; contract loans and discounts, which would reduce their bank notes in circulation (in 1814 this would include denying the hard-pressed Treasury further financial assistance); or call on correspondents to settle accounts in specie. The last alternative, being the least painful, was the first to be pursued. However effective under normal conditions, the cooperative agreements or understandings between correspondent banks could not withstand the pressure of an abrupt increase in the demand for specie by the public or one segment of the banking community. Just as the spirit of competition could not prevent collusive activities among banks, the same spirit of voluntarism was unable to insure the smooth functioning of the system when it was placed under a strain. The Treasury was in no position to aid the banks and even contributed to the problem. In its desperation to meet obligations, the government paid debts in whatever notes it had on hand. These were more often than not the notes of the Middle Atlantic banks. Such notes were already circulating at a discount in Boston, and the banks there immediately returned these obligations to the issuing institutions for redemption in coin.

Contemporary bankers, including Girard, seldom saw in such events as the specie crisis of 1814 a flaw in the banking system. They were more inclined to attribute their problems to the war with Britain, the antiwar sentiment of the New England bankers, the lack of cooperation among the banks, or, as Burrall confided to Simpson in July 1814, the fact that New York and Pennsylvania had chartered too many new banks given the available supply of specie. However faulty their perception of the causes, Girard and his fellow bankers were well aware of the consequences of a continued drain of specie.

With no sign of relief in sight, the banks of Philadelphia and the eastern seaboard were able to agree on one course of action—the general suspension of specie payments. On 1 September 1814 Simpson informed Burrall at the Bank of America that "encl^d is a Notice from the Banks in this City respecting the payment of Specie, from which you will see the impossibility of honoring your drafts in future, except in the current Bank notes of this City."[43] Philadelphia, and indeed most of the nation outside of New England, had been placed on a paper standard. Girard had no choice but to follow the lead of his competitors for to do otherwise would have invited a flood of demands for redemption of his outstanding notes and a virtual disappearance of his specie reserves.

The problem of how to settle interbank balances immediately arose. Unfortunately, the banks of the city found it easier to agree on suspension than on an acceptable way to attend to their mutual obligations. The Bank of North America took the lead and suggested a plan under which banks would agree to receive each other's notes and pay interest on the net balances. Balances would be limited under this plan, since banks would refuse to accept the notes of a bank whose indebtedness exceeded a previously determined amount. There was even a suggestion that joint meetings could be held on a weekly basis to equalize balances among banks. Although similar plans were adopted in other major cities, this proposal failed to gain approval in Philadelphia, and the city was without a mutual agreement for nearly a year after the decision to suspend.

Agreements reached in other cities, coupled with Girard's steadfast refusal to pay interest on deposits, placed him at a decided disadvantage. Burrall wrote to Simpson on 7 September 1814, confirming the suspension in New York and indicating that "the Banks here have agreed to pay interest on the balances due to and from each other."[44] Moreover, Burrall requested that, as the balances of the Bank of America in Girard's bank paid no interest, the former desired that remittances be made for the balance of their account as soon as possible. Again the weakness of the banking system was evident. At a time when increased cooperation and improved means of settling debts and making payments were clearly called for, the tendency was for institutions to contract interbank balances and thus reduce their ability to make interregional payments. Since the banks played a major role in the trade between regions, this curtailment in the means of payment threatened to add commercial disaster to financial contraction. In Girard's case, the contraction of deposits due other banks was spectacular—from $499,398 in 1814 to $9,110 in 1815. Over the same period, total interbank deposits declined from $551,571 to $121,795.[45]

The suspension also forced Girard to pay strict attention to his inland correspondents. Notes of Pennsylvania's country banks accumulated in Philadelphia institutions with little prospect of redemption in the immediate future. On 29 October the Farmer's Bank of Lancaster was informed that "The notes of your Bank have increased so much of late that we are obliged to decline them at present."[46] In lieu of specie settlements with the Farmer's Bank, Girard was willing to accept bank drafts on Philadelphia, Delaware, or New York to meet potential demands from these quarters. Unfortunately the Farmer's Bank was unable to supply such drafts.

As an alternative to the direct exchange of obligations, Girard and Simpson hit upon the idea of utilizing the correspondent relationship to settle accounts. The plan as conceived also indicated that Girard and his cashier were well versed in the usefulness of banker's balances. Simpson contacted John Heister, cashier of the Farmer's Bank of Reading, on 23 November, indicating Girard's desire to establish an account there and enclosing $6,000 ($5,000 in drafts on the Farmer's Bank of Lancaster and $1,000 in bank notes on the same institution). Simpson suggested that the institutions agree to receive each other's notes, since "we are frequently applied to for notes of your Bank, which we are in the habit of taking from our customers, but as the sums are small, it is more convenient if we could supply the demands by drafts on your Bank which would chiefly be to the mills in your neighborhood and might assist the circulation of your notes."[47]

Simpson revealed this strategy to Clendenin of the Farmer's Bank of Lancaster on 3 December. Noting that Girard still had some $30,000 worth of their notes, he indicated that between $15,000 and $20,000 of these would be remitted to the Farmer's Bank of Reading and placed at the credit of Stephen Girard's Bank. In this fashion, said Simpson, "we can easily pass drafts on that Bank and if this mode of remittance can be adopted it will facilitate the circulation of your paper in this City."[48] Under this arrangement all parties would benefit. The Farmer's Bank of Lancaster now found it easier to circulate its notes in Philadelphia; the Farmer's Bank of Reading had acquired an important new Philadelphia correspondent; and Girard now found it easier to dispose of inland bank notes and was better able to supply his Philadelphia customers with needed drafts. Thus while suspension weakened relations between some institutions, it also produced new and improved levels of cooperation between others.

The news of the peace concluded at Ghent was welcomed by all who had a stake or an interest in the nation's financial future. Secretary of the Treasury Dallas seized on this opportunity to simultaneously improve cooperation between the banks and the Treasury and move toward resumption. The first indication of this federal initiative came in a letter to Girard on 18 February 1815. In it, Dallas observed that "the change in our revenue which the peace will produce, enables us . . . to make fresh proposals to the Banks, and the monied men, as myself, I think secure the necessary accommodations for the Treasury." The secretary added, "I shall proceed to Philadelphia upon that business as soon as Congress adjourns."[49]

On 13 March Dallas laid out his plan of cooperation in the form of a Treasury circular to twenty-one banks along the eastern seaboard from Boston to Savannah. Girard's copy of the circular noted that "the restoration of peace, the revival of commerce, and the liberal provision made by Congress at the last session, for raising a permanent revenue from internal duties and taxes, will furnish the Treasury with ample means to meet all the demands upon it and to establish the public credit upon the surest foundation."[50] The advantages that Dallas indicated would accrue to participating banks were (1) they would have the privilege of funding Treasury notes, due and unpaid, on equal terms with others under the law[51]; (2) they would be the exclusive depository for public revenues; (3) their notes would be declared receivable in all payments to the United States; and (4) for loans made in anticipation of revenues, the direct tax and the duty on distilled spirits and stills might be specifically pledged to the banks that made temporary advances for the accommodation of the government. Dallas added that the Treasury required help presently in facilitating the transfer of public revenues from place to place, circulating new issues of Treasury notes, and anticipating public revenue to pay public debts of immediate urgency. "Upon these views," concluded Dallas, "I have deemed it a duty, frankly and cordially, to submit to your consideration the outline of a plan, which is designed in some degree, to connect State Banks . . . with each other and all of them with the Treasury, upon safe, beneficial and patriotic principles of association. The terms may be modified as to be rendered generally satisfactory; and the details can easily be thrown into form."

The plan itself contained ten basic points. Among these was the requirement that participating banks open accounts with each other "for the purpose of accommodating the Treasury in the manner hereafter stated." Specialized accounts were to be set up on the Treasury's behalf for specialized purposes, and drafts of the Treasury on any participating bank would be immediately received and credited to the specified account, "thus allowing the Treasury to transfer the public revenue from one place to another." In essence, if Girard had joined such an association, he would have been required to establish close relationships with the other Philadelphia banks, and they, in turn, would have been required to recognize his institution on a par with any other.

Girard's response to this initiative reveals his attitude toward cooperation. In no uncertain terms, he replied that "that part of your proposal which refers to association as its respects [sic] to open and keep accounts with the several State Banks which should accede to your plan, and also to receive their notes in payment, would be extremely inconvenient to me as a private Banker whose principal object is not to involve myself, but simply to manage the affairs of my Bank with that degree of prudence which will merit a general confidence."[52] In lieu of Dallas' proposal, Girard hinted at a different, smaller association of banks, presumably to accomplish the same ends. "Should you judge advisable to modify your plan," said Girard, "I will have no objection to associate my Banking Establishment as far as the interest of the United States will require, with two or three old Banks of this place also with the Planters' Bank of Savannah, the South Carolina Bank of Charleston, who I consider very good and extremely friendly to the administration and at New York with the Bank of America." It seems clear from this counterproposal that Girard felt more comfortable with an arrangement that would bind him to the older, more conservative members of the Philadelphia banking community and those institutions in the South with which he had a special relationship.

Dallas' reply was perhaps predictable. "The plan of the Treasury must necessarily be a general one," said the secretary, "and I regret very much that you cannot enter into it. You will at least accept the overture which has been made to you as proof of my official and personal confidence in you."[53] Girard's refusal to go along with the Treasury's plan was echoed by other prominent members of the financial community, and the proposed arrangement came to naught. If adopted, the Dallas plan would have constituted an interesting experiment in bank cooperation. The arrangement would have operated without the benefit of specie payments and stressed the mutual interdependence of the major banking institutions and their relationship with the Treasury. The ease with which the Treasury could have moved deposits from one bank or region to another would have given this scheme great flexibility, and the requirement that the government accept the notes of all participating banks would have contributed to the elimination of depreciated bank notes in some regions. Thus flexibility, safety, and uniformity in monetary affairs might have been achieved without a return to the use of gold and silver as the sole primary reserves of the banking system. In short, Dallas attempted to achieve, through voluntary cooperation, a system that closely resembled the operation of the national bank that he, Girard, and others were so ardently seeking. His failure in this endeavor indicated that resumption was a necessary precondition for the establishment of a national bank or a national banking system.

Suspension of specie payments did enable Girard to achieve the goal of having his bank designated a Treasury depository. Ironically, it was the lack of cooperation between the city institutions and Stephen Girard's Bank which had formed the principal obstacle. Since Girard kept no accounts at the other city banks, and since these institutions refused his notes, Treasury deposits made his bank vulnerable to specie raids like those following the loan of April 1813. Suspension made the presentation of Treasury drafts for specie payments impossible, and banks submitting such drafts would receive their own notes or the notes of other city banks.

The failure of Dallas' proposal for cooperation between the major banks and the Treasury put pressure on the Philadelphia banks to devise a scheme of their own for interbank settlements. Their system, which was to take effect in December 1815, included payment of interest on balances above $25,000, regular reporting of bank indebtedness, and the provision that banks could use local accounts to settle obligations, so long as all banks concerned were members of the agreement. Girard, as usual, was excluded from this agreement as well as the subsequent deliberations of the banks on resuming specie payments.

Just as the conditions created by the suspension of specie payments made possible the Girard bank's role as a federal depository, so too they laid the foundation for the first intracity account. Girard held large quantities of city bank notes even before suspension, as a protection against possible specie raids by the other city institutions. However, with the adoption of a paper standard in 1814, Girard's holdings of notes increased rapidly and stood at $1,152,318.15 by July 1816. With only $191,870.00 of his own notes in circulation, Girard was a net creditor of the city's banks by a substantial amount. As he was not a party to the agreement of the preceding fall, these net balances represented a significant loss of foregone interest income.

On 3 July, 1816 Girard contacted Jonathan Morton, president of the Bank of North America, concerning their obligations. "Having a considerable sum of your notes in my Banking house," said Girard, "I will thank you to inform me whether it will be agreeable to allow Interest on the amount thereof, or on such part as may be agreed on."[54] For their part, the board of directors of the Bank of North America reminded Girard that he was not a party to the city agreement and further charged that he had in the past refused to give the Bank of North America their own notes in payment, on the grounds that he could pay notes of any city bank.[55] The Board did offer, however, to call a meeting of the city banks to discuss admitting Girard to the agreement. Girard's reply marked a significant departure from his previous attitude toward cooperation. For the first time he indicated a willingness to establish permanent relationships with at least some of the city banks. He denied, of course, any deliberate attempt to deprive the Bank of North America of their notes and added, "I thank you for your offer to call a general committee of all the Banks, my object is not to keep an account with all those Money Institutions but simply with those with whom I have a good understanding."[56] He then added that "during the last eighteen months my Bank held constantly a considerable sum of your Bank Notes for which I have made no claim but the quantity having gradually increased to a sum of a greater magnitude, is the motive which had induced me to address you on the subject of Interest."

The situation was a delicate one, for reaching an accord with Girard in this matter would be tantamount to the formal recognition so long denied his bank. The Bank of North America was unwilling to assume this responsibility on its own and reiterated its desire to call a general meeting of all the banks. Girard held his ground, however, and expressed little interest in such a meeting until it was convenient for the Bank of North America to make arrangements regarding its notes.[57] "I do not intend to embarrass your Institution," said Girard, "but simply to obtain a part of what is reasonably due to me. Having a few hundred thousand dollars of your Bank Notes in the vaults of my Banking house . . . it is high time that some amicable arrangement respecting the Interest which I have claim from you, should take place, I therefore trust that by the 18th of the present Month, I will receive a satisfactory answer to this and former application." This ultimatum, delivered on 16 July, gave the Bank of North America two days to bring forward an acceptable proposal. The Bank of North America acceded, and Girard's account with that institution commenced on 5 August 1816. At that time Girard's bank was credited with $200,000. On 3 September interest payments of $2000 were made for July and August; an equal payment on 4 November; and a final interest payment on 26 February 1817.[58]

When the Philadelphia banks resumed specie payments on 20 February 1817, the account with the Bank of North America was continued. The solid front of resistance to Stephen Girard's Bank had been broken, and by year's end accounts had been established at the Commercial Bank of Pennsylvania, the Schuylkill Bank, the Mechanic's Bank, the Philadelphia Bank, and the Farmer's and Mechanic's Bank.[59] In later years accounts were added with the Southwark Bank, the Kensington Bank, and the Bank of Penn Township.[60]

To some extent Girard's recognition by the city banks was guaranteed by the establishment of the Bank of the United States in Philadelphia. As a major stockholder and one of the principal architects of the BUS, Girard was bound to have close and amicable relations with the new national bank. Once recognized as a legitimate member of the banking community by so powerful an institution as the BUS, Stephen Girard's Bank would command the respect of competitors. Thus nearly five years after commencing operations, Stephen Girard's Bank became a full-fledged member of the Philadelphia banking community. This change in status resulted in major changes in the bank's operations. As table 9 clearly illustrates, Girard's business began to assume a more local character. Before 1816 all deposits by other banks were with non-Philadelphia institutions. However, starting in 1816, the majority of those banker's balances were with Philadelphia banks. The proportion of city deposits averaged nearly 71 percent between 1816 and 1831.

The period of suspension had forced the nation's banks to focus on

Table 9

Distribution of banker's balances
Stephen Girard's Bank

Date (1 October)	Philadelphia banks	Other banks
1812	— %	100.0%
1813	—	100.0
1814	—	100.0
1815	—	100.0
1816	96.8	3.2
1817	17.8	82.2
1818	82.1	17.9
1819	53.3	46.7
1820	54.3	45.7
1821	43.4	56.6
1822	54.3	45.7
1823	62.8	37.2
1824	95.3	4.7
1825	62.0	38.0
1826	78.4	21.6
1827	90.7	9.3
1828	96.3	3.7
1829	72.1	27.9
1830	89.5	10.5
1831	83.5	16.5

Source: SGC, II, 393–94.

the problems associated with increasing interdependence. The resumption of specie payments brought with it the establishment of the Second Bank of the United States but no fundamental reform of the banking system. Girard's bank correspondence betwen 1817 and 1831 reveals the same problems of remittances, specie shortages, and the settlement of balances that plagued the bank in the early years of its existence. However, the hostility of previous years appears to have been forgotten, and Girard's relations with the city banks improved steadily after 1817. Just how far that cooperation had proceeded by 1825 is evident in a letter from Joseph Roberts, Girard's new cashier, to George Newbold of the Bank of America.[61] The latter bank had been using drafts on Girard's bank to settle its accounts with the Schuylkill Bank, which, in turn, demanded specie from Girard. Roberts admonished Newbold for this practice and noted that "there has been for some time back a large balance suffered to remain between the Banks here . . . and latterly a very good understanding has subsisted between us Bankers—It is rather unpleasant to have that harmony disturbed."[62]

The characterization of Girard as an interloper dissolved over time, but the price of acceptance was a certain loss of independence in the bank's operations. During the last decade of its existence, Stephen Girard's Bank, at least on the surface, was nearly indistinguishable from its chartered competition. What remained unique were the character and philosophy of Girard himself. The principles that governed the decision-making process at Stephen Girard's Bank were clearly those of its founder and chief operator.

6

Institutional Philosophy

The unique quality of Stephen Girard's Bank did not reside in the nature of its ownership or its mode of operation. Private banking had a well-established history long before the nineteenth century, and, as we have seen, Girard's bank came to resemble the other Philadelphia institutions in most external respects. What set Girard's bank apart was its hybrid character, which incorporated some of the basic features of both European and American banking. Moreover, Girard's own philosophy of banking and finance was uniquely compatible with the nature of his banking house.

The great European merchant bankers were largely a product of the search for an outlet for accumulated capital. Such capital was most often the result of prior mercantile activity, which was frequently continued simultaneously with the firm's lending activities. Only in rare cases did such European houses specialize in purely financial activities. American banks, on the other hand, were the result of a great demand for capital to finance a growing number of commercial operations and to help provide fixed and social-overhead capital. In the process of lending, American banks, unlike their European counterparts, issued debt instruments in the form of bank notes and deposits, which became a principal element of the nation's money supply.

In practice, the European merchant bankers often acted as rationers or auctioners of loanable funds, while the rapidly growing American banking system was increasingly performing those functions associated with modern financial intermediaries. The essence of this intermediary

90

function was to make possible the process of indirect finance by issuing indirect debt in the form of bank liabilities to borrowers, and receiving in return the direct debt of merchants, farmers, and manufacturers in the form of bills of exchange, mortgages, and accommodation paper. The nearly constant debate over which groups should have access to this process of credit creation should not obscure the very real difference that characterized the American banking system.

Stephen Girard's Bank was solidly based on a large proportion of its founder's mercantile fortune. Indeed, the bank's initial capital represented those assets that Girard was able to repatriate from Europe in the wake of the Napoleonic wars. Like the Continental and British merchant bankers, Girard sought a profitable employment for his accumulated wealth, and its subsequent capitalization in the form of a private bank was by no means the only option open to him. Once he had chosen to become a banker, Girard could have followed the traditional path of merchant banking, remaining out of public view and utilizing the facilities of the city's chartered banks when necessary. That he did not is significant. Girard chose instead to emulate the commercial banks in nearly all respects, including the issue of bank notes. Perhaps of equal significance is the fact that Girard commenced his banking activities at a time when the legislature was clearly moving in the direction of outlawing even limited banking functions for nonchartered institutions. Underlying those decisions and the policies of his bank was Girard's philosophy of banking. It is a difficult philosophy to characterize for a variety of reasons. Girard was reluctant to philosophize, and enjoyed stating that "my deeds must be my life," so that any consideration of his banking philosophy must be largely inferential. In addition, it is well to remember that Girard had a multiplicity of commercial and financial interests. His bank was by no means the sole claimant on his time or energy, and it is often difficult to separate his views in one area from those in another. On the other hand, any attempt to analyze the operations of Stephen Girard's Bank without an investigation of the founder's principles would be incomplete.

There is little evidence that Stephen Girard knew a great deal about the internal operations of commercial banking institutions when he founded his own establishment. However, in an era when even the most knowledgable businessmen had not yet grasped the full potential of commercial banking, such relative ignorance may have been a minor handicap. Moreover, Girard had been shrewd enough to acquire the services of George Simpson, the cashier of the late Bank of the United States, to perform a similar function in his own bank. Because of Girard's lack of experience and his early tendency to relegate daily decision making to Simpson, the latter's role was crucial during the first years of the bank. As time wore on, however, Girard devoted more and more time to his banking enterprise, and after Simpson's death in 1822, his views were clearly dominant.

To a large extent the policies of the older, chartered banks of the city, such as the Bank of North America and the Bank of Pennsylvania, also reflected the views of the prominent leaders of the commercial community who made up their boards of directors. Such banks often tended to ignore the credit needs of the agricultural and industrial sectors, preferring the relative safety and familiarity of purely commercial lending. The prominence of short-term commercial paper in the portfolios of these institutions reflected the orthodox view of commercial banking in the early nineteenth century, a view that was already subject to attack.

A new generation of banks, arising in the second decade of the nineteenth century, moved to fill this deficiency in the Philadelphia capital market. The Mechanic's Bank and the Farmer's and Mechanic's Bank, as their names implied, were directed by a different group of entrepreneurs. While not averse to commercial lending, such banks were less selective in terms of their clientele and more prone to engage in unsecured accommodation loans. In this divergence of views, Girard's innate conservatism led him to favor the practices of the older banks. It appears that Girard was as much an adherent of the "real bills" doctrine, or commercial loan theory of banking, as the institutions that so bitterly opposed his operations. There is little or no evidence that the enmity of the Philadelphia banks had a basis in divergent banking philosophies; indeed, the directors of any of the city's leading institutions would have found little to quarrel with in Girard's statement that "the principle of Banking is not to furnish capital but simply to facilitate commercial operations by discounting bills or notes which result from real transactions for which value has been received."[1] Nor would most take issue with the assertion that "the operations of a Bank should resemble that of a fountain which receives and turns out."[2] Both statements mirrored the widely held contemporary view of the passive role of commercial banks. The banking system would thus reflect the level of commercial activity, contracting or expanding the supply of credit in concert with the underlying rhythm of the economy. It was this philosophy that led to the tendency of commercial bank activity to accentuate movements in the business cycle, providing ample credit to fuel the booms and contracting rapidly in response to a downswing.

Much of this attitude can be attributed to the banker's concern for safety, soundness, or, as Girard phrased it, "prudence." Specialization in short-term commercial lending allowed for quick liquidation in recessions by a severe restriction of new banking. Girard's attention to the prudent operation of his bank was evident from its very inception. He began operations with a very large capital, amounting to more than one million dollars. This rose quickly to $1,304,881.38 by the end of 1812, and through regular and substantial additions stood at $1.5 million on 1 January 1814; $1.8 million on 1 January 1816; $2.5 million by mid-1822; and $3 million by January 1827.[3] These additions to the bank's capital came first from the diversion of interest and discount income from profits and loss into capital stock, and later (1822 and 1827) by transfer from surplus to capital stock.[4] Moreover, Girard's initial capital was paid-in capital and was represented on the asset side by a substantial proportion of highly liquid items and cash. In contrast, the corporate banks almost always commenced operations long before authorized capital had been paid in by the stockholders.

Girard's philosophy of prudence is to some extent evident in an examination of the ratio of the capital to demand liabilities, which is designed to provide a rough indication of the owner's contribution to the debts of the bank. Because the modern bank's capital plays little role in the safety of its operations, this ratio is generally well below 10 percent. However, in the early ninetenth century, an institution's capital played a major role in the safety of its continued operations. Included in demand liabilities are individual deposits, deposits due other banks, and bank notes in circulation. This measure takes on added interest in Girard's case, since the charters of his competitors often set limits on the ratio of total indebtedness to capital, while he was free to pursue a policy appropriate to his own philosophy.[5]

An additional measure of bank safety utilizing the capital account is the ratio of capital to total assets. This proportion indicates the percentage by which the institution's assets may decline in value before losses are incurred by those holding the bank's indirect debt instruments (that is, bank notes and deposits). Table 10 presents both ratios for Stephen Girard's Bank and the average Pennsylvania bank in the years for which sufficient data are available.

As the figures clearly show, the Girard bank never approached the rough equality of debts and capital so common among the chartered banks of the state. By maintaining such a high ratio and keeping a sizable proportion of his assets, in highly liquid form, particularly during the bank's early years, Girard was prepared at nearly all times to meet the demand of depositors or noteholders. The capital/asset ratio for Girard's bank also reflected a low risk preference, one shared by the other Philadelphia institutions. The values in table 10 are extremely high by modern standards, perhaps reflecting the nineteenth-century

Institutional Philosophy

Table 10
Capital ratios of Stephen Girard's
Bank and the average Pennsylvania bank

Date[a]	Capital/demand liabilities		Capital/assets	
	Stephen Girard's Bank	*Average Pennsylvania bank*	*Stephen Girard's Bank*	*Average Pennsylvania bank*
1812	—	—	.50	—
1813	—	—	—	—
1814	—	—	—	—
1815	1.77	—	.46	—
1816	2.22	—	.40	—
1817	2.62	—	.57	—
1818	3.39	—	.59	—
1819	3.70	1.77	.62	.61
1820	3.23	1.50	.60	.60
1821	2.99	1.06	.60	.50
1822	3.35	1.18	.64	.54
1823	3.54	1.31	.63	.56
1824	2.78	1.17	.58	.52
1825	5.42	.97	.66	.48
1826	4.40	1.02	.66	.50
1827	4.49	.87	.66	.47
1828	5.59	.85	.70	.43
1829	6.34	.92	.72	.49
1830	5.79	.82	.72	.46
1831	—	.78	.68	.44
Average	3.85	1.09	.61	.51

Sources: SGC, II, 393, 394, and J. Van Fenstermaker, *The Development of Commercial Banking 1782–1837* (Kent, Ohio, 1965), pp. 224–25.

a. Girard bank data as of 1 October of reporting year. Pennsylvania bank data as of first Monday in November of reporting year.

desire to guard against the precipitous and frequent declines that characterized the contemporary market for financial instruments. It should be noted, however, that the tendency of authorized capital to exceed paid-in capital had the effect of artificially inflating this ratio. The noticeable decline in the capital/asset ratio for the average Pennsylvania bank is absent from the Girard bank data because of Girard's preference for expanding the bank's capital account prior to a major expansion of demand liabilities by loans and investments. Accordingly, expansion of total loans followed expansion of the bank's capital stock in 1816, 1822, and 1827. This tendency is also visible in Girard's often repeated desire to increase the "active capital" of his bank. The decline in the ratio for the average Pennsylvania bank may indicate a decline in the perceived risk of a financial panic in a period when capital markets were becoming more efficient.

Another touchstone of banking philosophy was the institution's decision on the structure of reserves. Girard, like other bankers, preferred earning assets to cash reserves in the form of specie and bank notes. On the other hand, a sudden demand for gold and silver by the bank's depositors or noteholders could place a great strain on the institution's specie supply and force a quick liquidation of earning assets. Other banks could exert the same kind of pressure through the periodic presentation of bank notes for redemption in specie, or by calling on correspondents for deposits in the form of specie. The latter situation was more likely to occur when the patterns of trade and finance produced a chronic specie flow from one region of the country to another.[6]

Table 11 summarizes the cash reserves of Stephen Girard's Bank as a percentage of total assets and compares these results with the same data for an average Pennsylvania bank. The early years of the Girard bank's operation were characterized by a relatively high ratio of cash reserves to total assets. This ratio fell from nearly 60 percent in 1812 to about 25 percent by 1823 and stood at only 16 percent in 1831. The ratio for Girard's bank exceeded that for the average Pennsylvania bank until 1825, when the situation was reversed.

Of greater interest than the simple change in the size of the bank's reserves is their level relative to certain key liabilities. Perhaps the most scrutinized ratio in this regard is the proportion of specie reserves to bank notes in circulation. This concept can be broadened to include all demand liabilities. Early banking establishments in the United States were constantly forced to tread a fine line between profits and insolvency. The creation of loans or other income-earning assets involved the creation of demand liabilities—bank notes or deposits—which could be redeemed in specie. While the creation of demand liabilities through the process of lending might be limited by the bank's charter, this was seldom the real limiting factor. On a practical basis, the bank's ability to support a given volume of bank notes and deposits was a function of its specie reserves and the velocity with which such liabilities were returned to the issuing institution. Some banks adopted policies or tactics to minimize the redemption of their obligations and thus permit them to acquire a maximum volume of loans on the basis of a minimum supply of specie. Such tactics included lending in areas distant from the bank

Table 11

Cash as a percentage of total assets, Stephen Girard's Bank
and the average Pennsylvania bank

Date[a]	Stephen Girard's Bank	Average Pennsylvania bank
1812	.599	—
1813	—	—
1814	—	—
1815	.384	—
1816	.395	—
1817	.315	—
1818	.259	—
1819	.355	.129
1820	.406	.182
1821	.374	.224
1822	.272	.183
1823	.231	.161
1824	.245	.205
1825	.184	.226
1826	.223	.201
1827	.177	.197
1828	.168	.183
1829	.136	.184
1830	.173	.243
1831	.160	.187
Average	.280	.207

Sources: SGC, II, 393–94, and Van Fenstermaker, *Development of American Commercial Banking*, p. 224.

a. Girard bank data as of 1 October of reporting year. Pennsylvania bank data as of first Monday in November of reporting year.

itself, making redemption of notes difficult and expensive; issuing large numbers of small denomination notes, whose individual redemption was not worth the effort; issuing post notes which were payable in specie on or after a stated date in the future; or separating the loan office from the redemption office, with the latter located in an inaccessible region, the practice of the infamous but numerically insignificant wildcat banks. Such tactics were more often characteristic of rural or "country" banks, whose meager specie reserves induced the adoption of such practices.

Because of a greater degree of cooperation among institutions and a large supply of specie, the Philadelphia banks were under less pressure to inhibit the velocity of redemption in normal times. A variety of rules of thumb were used to maintain what was considered a proper ratio between specie reserves and bank notes in circulation. Perhaps the most widely accepted ratio was 3 to 1, or three dollars in bank notes for each one in specie reserves.[7] Nor was the reserve ratio which a bank maintained independent of its loan policy. Should the institution favor short-term (for example, thirty-to-sixty-day) loans of a commercial nature, its entire portfolio could be liquidated in a very short time. Such an institution might feel comfortable with a lower reserve ratio than another bank that held a high proportion of long-term, illiquid, and unshiftable loans as assets. An ample supply of short-term commercial paper and a fairly well-developed market in financial instruments made it possible for Philadelphia banks to operate safely with much lower reserve ratios than their rural counterparts.

In contrast Girard's conservative philosophy and fear of specie raids by his competitors led him to maintain reserves far in excess of the norm. Table 12 compares the reserve ratios of Stephen Girard's Bank with those of the average Pennsylvania institution. These figures, coupled with evidence in the bank correspondence, indicate that Girard attempted to maintain a minimum 100 percent specie reserve against bank notes in circulation. Girard's contemporary biographer maintained that "his specie responsibility always far exceeded, even in a compound ratio, that of other institutions." Referring to this policy, the biographer asserted that during the unsettled years following the Panic of 1819, Girard maintained sufficient specie reserves to satisfy not only holders of the bank's notes but all holders of demand liabilities; Girard "never semed to evince any great anxiety as to the small or large amount of application for discounts. If the offerings were limited, he was content to keep his surplus funds, and draw specie from the other banks, to stock his vaults for emergencies."[8] Thus the slackened demand for loans and discounts following the Panic of 1819 probably accounts for the inflated ratio of specie to total demand liabilities during those years. Moreover, in periods when full specie backing for bank notes in circulation seemed threatened, Girard quickly took measures to restore this parity. In 1816 Girard curtailed the circulation of bank notes and purchased gold to correct a reserve ratio which had fallen to nearly 50 percent.[9] In 1827 George Newbold, cashier of the Bank of America, requested Stephen Girard's Bank to remit specie for obligations due. Girard demurred, indicating that loans had increased so considerably that "our liabilities are not nearly equal to our specie means."[10] Later in 1828 Girard reduced the bank's holdings of 6 percent stock and paid a premium for Spanish gold, so that by 1830 specie reserves once again exceeded bank notes in circulation.[11]

Perhaps predictably, Girard's attitude toward post notes was some-

Institutional Philosophy

Table 12

Reserve ratios of
Stephen Girard's Bank and the
average Pennsylvania bank

	Specie/bank note		Specie/demand liabilities	
	Stephen	Average	Stephen	Average
	Girard's	Pennsylvania	Girard's	Pennsylvania
Date[a]	Bank	bank	Bank	bank
1814	1.732	—	—	—
1815	.640	.070	.171	—
1816	4.445	.169	.842	—
1817	2.303	.230	.415	—
1818	1.317	.201	.362	—
1819	4.648	.409	1.002	.200
1820	4.663	.493	1.207	.229
1821	3.902	.488	1.000	.214
1822	1.520	.351	.510	.187
1823	1.311	.459	.395	.201
1824	3.096	.429	.548	.198
1825	1.083	.444	.349	.199
1826	2.851	.380	.583	.170
1827	—	.338	—	.151
1828	1.160	.289	.299	.136
1829	.642	.323	.204	.157
1830	1.355	.382	.403	.172
1831	—	.307	—	.140
Average	2.291	.338	.521	.181

Sources: SGC, II, 393, 394; Van Fenstermaker, *Development of Commercial Banking*, pp. 224–25; and *A Statistical Summary of the Commercial Banks Incorporated in the U.S. Prior to 1819* (Kent, Ohio, 1965), pp. 19–20.

a. Girard Bank data as of 1 October of reporting year. Pennsylvania bank data as of first Monday in November of reporting year.

what cool, as he was particularly suspicious of activity that might cast doubts on the integrity of his bank. When these were issued, Girard apparently preferred to draw such notes to bearer and utilize them as a form of cashier's check or draft. In 1827 John Barr of Baltimore was told that "I can draw you Post Notes in your favor from $100 to $1,000 at 30 days or longer—Our large notes paid at the counter are to bearer."[12] Girard added that "with respect to post notes we seldom issue them, only on special occasions." Moreover, indicated Girard, his bank would issue no post notes in denominations over $1,000 and no interest would be paid on the notes during the time for which they were drawn.[13] As table 13 indicates, only a portion of the post notes issued were in circulation at any one time, and by the mid-1820s the bank began to substitute large-denomination bank notes of $500 and $1,000 in their place. It seems reasonable to conclude that when Girard issued post notes, it was with the convenience of the bank's customers in mind.

Most reflective of Girard's banking philosophy were the bank's lending policies. Essentially Girard dealt with three broadly defined categories of borrowers—individual borrowers; federal, state, and local governments; and a group of noncommercial, private companies largely concerned with the provision of social-overhead capital. Over time, Girard's attitude toward the latter two categories underwent some degree of change while he remained steadfast in his philosophy of individual lending.

The bank's first and only major involvement with the federal Treasury was its participation in the $16 million loan of April 1813. While Girard's holdings of federal debt remained substantial for several years following the War of 1812, there was a persistent decline over time in their importance relative to total assets. In part the declining importance of government stock was a result of the reduction in new issues following the war and in part a result of a change in Girard's attitude toward direct participation in Treasury loan operations. The specie raids of Philadelphia banks and the brief but bitter exchange with the Treasury that followed participation in the 1813 loan left their mark on Girard. He refused to join with Astor and Parish in a syndicate to purchase a substantial block of the $25 million loan of 1814, despite a well-conceived and highly profitable arrangement with the Treasury. Even the pleas for financial assistance of his friend, Secretary of the Treasury Alexander J. Dallas, went unheeded. Only two weeks after assuming his post at the Treasury, Dallas wrote Girard requesting a loan of $283,526 to meet the government's debts in Philadelphia. In addition, Dallas requested Girard to renew any Treasury notes which he held in his bank and which were due. "I would not ask," said Dallas, "if I were not convinced of your friendly disposition. . . ."[14] Girard was quick to note that he had the greatest confidence in government security, "yet having already far upwards of $1,500,000 of United States Stock locked up in my Bank, my present resources do not permit me to go further."[15] Despite the Secretary's persistent pleas, Girard was adamant. "I have examined the state of my finances," he said, "and with the best disposition to comply with your request I find it impractical."[16]

By year's end the Treasury faced another crisis, this time in Boston. The banks of Boston had not suspended specie payments, and the bank notes of non-specie-paying institutions circulated there at depreciated rates. The problem, to put it simply, was that the Treasury owed debts in Boston and needed gold, silver, or Boston bank notes to honor these at face value. Dallas contacted Girard privately on 5 December and indicated, "I wish to place the sum of 315,000 dollars in Boston to pay the dividend on the public debt becoming due there on the first of January next. Can you assist me in this operation and on what terms will you do it?"[17] Girard's reply noted that he was unable to assist in meeting the dividends, for "it is the duty of the public creditors to wait for interest or receive Treasury notes."[18]

Despite these rebuffs, Dallas persisted in his attempts to solicit funds from Girard. On 7 April 1815 Girard received a communication from the Treasury indicating the secretary's desire to "anticipate the public revenue" by some three or four hundred thousand dollars. The loan was to be repaid in twelve months and draw 6 percent interest.[19] Girard's answer was to the point. "You knowing my disposition on that subject, I take the liberty to observe to you, that while the drafts of the Treasurer will be remitted to any one of the Banks of this City who will refuse to receive payment in notes of my Bank, or will retain said draft until they accumulate to a sum of magnitude, it will be imprudent to make a Contract which will promote the Interest of a Company Bank and embarrass my Banking Operations."[20] In spite of Girard's apparent disinclination to come to the assistance of the government, Dallas offered assurances. "If you should agree to the loan proposed in my letter of the 7th instant, the drafts of the Treasury will not be sent to the Bankers of Philadelphia, but will be passed in payments to public officers, or individuals for such sums and at such times, as will be made convenient to you."[21] Despite such pledges of good faith, Girard could not be moved.

It is difficult to determine whether Girard's sudden coolness toward government lending represented a basic change in his view of the proper relationship between banks and the Treasury or simply a determination to avoid the problems associated with the 1813 loan. It does seem fairly clear, however, from his active participation in the establishment of the Second Bank of the United States that Girard came to regard a national bank as the proper instrument to assist in Treasury financing.

Contemporary reports to the contrary, Girard's bank did not carry a large portfolio of state or Philadelphia debt. City bonds appear on the books from 1812 to 1820, when they amounted to only $2,200. Likewise, Pennsylvania debt appears only between 1827 and 1831, and New

York State 6 percents are recorded for one year only (1824) and valued at $7,500.[22]

Girard's only important departure from the "real bills" lending policy in the private sector involved loans to four transportation companies. The Ridge Turnpike Company received $10,000 in March 1813; the Schuyl-kill Navigation Company received $260,850 over a three-year period from 1824 to 1827; the Mount Carbon Railroad received $30,000 in October 1830; and the Danville and Pottsville Railroad Company received $20,000 in May 1831.[23] Since Girard's avowed philosophy of banking left little room for such long-term provision of capital, we must assume some change of position over time.

Leaving such exceptions aside, Girard's attitude toward loans to in-dividuals exhibited a remarkable degree of consistency throughout the bank's history, and his tendency to concentrate on short-term com-mercial paper outstripped that of even his most conservative competi-tors. Girard was apparently aware of this difference, for on 4 February 1813 Simpson described the bank as being "differently situated from other Banks having in view only the accommodation of [its] customers in the discounting of notes of real business."[24] More than a decade later, William Green and W. H. Harrison were informed that only "business paper" or "business notes" formed a basis for loans at Stephen Girard's Bank.[25]

As one who believed strongly in the essential correctness of the bills-only philosophy, Girard was not reluctant to admonish those institu-tions that departed from its precepts. Shortly after the resumption of specie payments in March 1817, John Stoney of Charleston lamented the shortage of money in that city. Girard's reply was pointed. "I am extremely sorry," he said "to observe the scarcity of money with you which in my opinion should only be attributed to the conduct of your bank which in view to a good dividend have adopted the maxim to discount accommodation notes which are renewed when in maturity by which means their capital is out of their reach and they are prevented to relieve the most industrious clan of your merchants by discounting paper which results from sales and other transactions for which value has been received."[26]

As if his bills-only policy were not restrictive enough, Girard at-tempted to restrict loans geographically to residents of Philadelphia, and it appears that few exceptions were made. One disappointed customer was a well-known Quaker merchant, Jacob Barker of New York. "I regret that my nonresidence precludes my having discounts at thy Bank," he wrote, "but for that I might supply large sums in good paper and be accommodated by the money."[27] This rigid policy was still in effect in 1823, when J. B. Richardson was informed that "this Bank only lends on Personal Security and that confined to the City."[28] When rare exceptions to this rule were made, the paper discounted required the signatures of two Philadelphia merchants or collateral.

Some banks of the period attempted to reap the rewards of accommodation lending without sacrificing the appearance of soundness. To accomplish this, short-term loans would be made with the understanding that renewals would be granted at the expiration of the original note. Thus what appeared to be short-term, commercial credit was in fact intermediate or long-term accommodation lending. Girard would have none of such practices and consistently eschewed renewals. For example, on 30 November 1816, Joshua M. Wallace was informed that "the loan made to you on the notes of J. B. Wallace was not intended to be continued by renewals and . . . payment will be expected from the drawer of the said notes received as Coll¹ security as they shall become due."[29]

Girard was equally opposed to granting renewals to noncommercial borrowers. When the Schuylkill Navigation Company's notes for some $230,850 fell due between March and September of 1824, the firm asked for a renewal. "The extension of time which you require," replied Girard, "and fix to seven or eight months will greatly derange the plan of my money operations. I am under the necessity to decline granting your request in hope you will be able to obtain the necessary accommodation through some other channel, but should you be disappointed, I will endeavor to meet your view as far as reasonable."[30] Not only did Girard relent in this instance, but there was some indication that previous renewals had been granted. On 2 May 1826 Roberts informed Joseph Lewis, president of the Schuylkill Navigation Company, that "I am directed by Mr. Girard to inform the Board of Managers, that he agrees to their resolve of the 1st inst. of extending the Loan of $230,850 for three periods of 60 days each of the notes from time when they respectively fall due under the 7th and last agreement.[31] The Ridge Turnpike Company also received some consideration, for on 12 August 1816 Simpson told the president and managers of the company that "I am directed to inform you that it is expected that the Bond on which you obtained a loan of $10,000 from this Bank 5 January, 1813 payable in six months will be discharged and paid off on or before the 5th January next as it is not convenient for Mr. Girard to continue the loan beyond that period."[32]

The pressure for renewal of individual notes became so great in 1816 that, according to Stephen Simpson, a new rule was adopted to insure that all borrowers were aware that no renewal of a note was ever to be made.[33] Moreover, when a renewal was unavoidable, additional endorsers or collateral were required. Benjamin Williams was reminded in 1824 that his notes had been deposited as collateral security and that "it was only in consequence thereof that a renewal of your note without another Indorser would take place."[34]

Some flexibility in the bank's loan policy was necessary, and this manifested itself in the maturity and interest-rate structure of the bank's loans and discounts. Girard's original intention to limit loans and discounts to paper with a maximum of sixty days to maturity soon went by the board. It was more convenient to adjust the maturity structure to match changes in customer demand and fluctuations in the economy. On 4 January 1813 Simpson informed his counterpart at the Mechanic's Bank of Baltimore, D. A. Smith, that two notes that ran twelve and fifteen months respectively were "too long" and are not discounted as Mr. Girard limits his discounts to 4 months."[35] However, by 26 August 1815, T. M. Forman was told that "the custom of this Bank is to lend money for 60 or 90 days on negotiable notes to such persons as keep accounts with us and that payment is always expected at maturity without renewal."[36] In July 1823 Roberts announced that notes of from "sixty to one hundred days" were discounted at Girard's Bank.[37] This same policy was in effect on 29 January 1824, but by April of the same year it had changed once more.[38] On the latter date, in response to a request by W. H. Harrison for a fifteen-hundred-dollar loan for one year, Roberts replied that the "loans made by this Bank [are] confined to business paper exclusively of from 90 to 120 days."[39] A letter to John T. Barr of Baltimore on 12 March 1828 indicated that the four-month limit was still in force.[40] By September 1829 the limit on repayment had been raised to "6 months or 180 days," and two years later, on 27 September 1831, Roberts announced that Girard had decided that morning to discount notes of five months or less.[41] Under almost all circumstances, loans to individuals were characterized by a maximum term of no more than six months and frequently less.

His ability to finely tune loan policy and his willingness to forgo present profits for long-run advantages distinguished Girard's operations from those of most chartered institutions. The decentralized decision making that characterized the boards of other banks precluded such flexibility; they were under constant pressure to produce adequate dividends at regular intervals and were often forced to pursue high-risk loan policies to accomplish this end. The advantage that Girard enjoyed in this respect is evident in a letter from Jonathan Burrall on 21 January 1814. The New Yorker explained the difficulty that the Bank of

America was experiencing in meeting the demand for specie. "Our loans to contractors and others made when there was but little demand for discounts "are a great proportion of them, on paper having a long time to run, which make it difficult to contract discounts very suddenly, particularly when the other Banks are drawing in and therefore we cannot liquidate accounts with the other Banks, in this way, immediately."[42] The harried cashier added that "our course in making loans on long paper was contrary to my judgement—but the desire of making good dividends and impatience of seeing any means lie idle, was too strong for me to arrest it, altho I foresaw that difficult times for Banks were coming on." By contrast, Girard, who was under similar pressures, was able to contract loans and discounts by more than 45 percent, from $1,121,268.41 on 1 January 1814 to $611,486.83 on 1 July 1814.[43]

The flexibility of maturity limits also served a significant function as a rationing device for loanable funds. A Pennsylvania regulation limiting interest rates to 6 percent per annum made necessary a variety of alternative rationing mechanisms during periods of intense demand for credit or retrenchment by lending institutions. Another rationing device that reflected Girard's personal philosophy was the requirement that borrowers at his bank also maintain a deposit there. On this issue Girard and Simpson did not see eye to eye. From the very beginning of the bank's operations, the latter believed that "a fair running account was considered sufficient to entitle a creditable applicant to liberal accommodations," and the "amount of deposits was not regarded by him as an absolute scale upon which to graduate and apportion discounts." Girard, on the other hand, felt strongly that "the scale of deposits ought to be the ratio of loans."[44]

The practice could be viewed as a way to maintain average balances of depositors at as high a level as possible in order to circumvent the restrictions imposed by the state's usury laws. Girard may also have felt that reputable merchants should possess adequate supplies of working capital for normal business and should borrow only to meet peak demands.[45] Whatever the principal motive, depositors were expected to maintain idle balances in order to insure that their loan or discount applications would meet with success. Simpson's opposition to this policy was based on the assumption that "to act on a regular balance sheet . . . in the loaning of money, is to encourage and entice the artful, to practice the deposit for the sake of the loan, reckless of the ability, as well as the intention of final payment." Girard's policy, maintained Simpson, "sowed the seeds of many spurious accounts, which afterwards involved . . . considerable losses."[46] In the early years of the bank's operations Simpson's position carried great weight. Girard was, after all, new to the banking profession and moreover was often too busy with outside interests to exert firm control over the day-to-day operations of his establishment. Only after Simpson's demise in 1822 was Girard able to completely dominate the loan policy of the bank. According to Simpson's son, after the death of his father Girard "adopted the plan of graduating discounts upon deposits."[47]

Some quantitative evidence supports the contention that Girard's system was incorporated over time. If the policy of granting loans on the basis of the borrower's account at the bank was strictly adhered to, we should expect to find a similarity between the distribution of loans by size and the distribution of deposits. Table 13 indicates that in 1812,

Table 13
Distribution of loans and
deposits, 1812 and 1831

Date	Over $1,000		Under $1,000	
	Deposits	*Loans*	*Deposits*	*Loans*
1812	24%	47%	76%	53%
1831	19%	22%	81%	78%

Source: See Chapter 7, *tables* 25 and 26.

24 percent of deposits and 47 percent of loans were over $1,000. By 1831, 19 percent of deposits and 22 percent of loans fell into this category. For loans and deposits under $1,000, the same pattern emerges. Deposits in this category constituted 76 percent of the total in 1812, and loans 53 percent, while the comparable figures for 1831 were 81 percent and 78 percent respectively. Quite clearly the distribution of deposits and loans coincided more closely in 1831 than in 1812. Moreover, the change over time was accomplished by a large shift in the distribution of deposits. This suggests that Girard's views increasingly prevailed and loans were brought more closely into line with deposits.

The policy of requiring prospective customers to maintain accounts at his bank did not always endear Girard to his fellow merchants of the city. A case in point is George Harrison, the navy agent in Philadelphia, who subscribed to $45,000 of the $16 million loan in 1813.[48] Harrison was directed to pay the $45,000 at Girard's bank on 15 April. Assuming that his reputation was sufficient collateral to discount notes, he informed Simpson on 9 April, "I shall pay into your Bank on the 15th— $45,000 cash Hook or by crook—will Croesus discount for me approved paper payable this month $ 3,000

May	29,000
June 15	6,000
Aug 11	3,500
Sept 13	4,000
	$45,000

I must have your official reply, and intend to call for it in person be-tween 11 and 12."[49]

Simpson returned Harrison's note with the following remarks: "Mr. G. would not determine previously upon the discount of any paper—but it will depend on the merits of the accounts of the applicants at the time of the offering." Harrison's reply of the same day pointedly reflected his opinion of Girard's policy. "I *am* and *always have been* well disposed toward G. and his Bank and in truth I have only been awaiting an opportunity to open an account with you—but my friend, I will *not be dragooned* into it and I regret that my application should depend on the merits of my account at the time of offering."[50] It should be noted in passing that Harrison recovered sufficiently to submit, on 15 April, checks totalling $45,012 for $51,150 of government stock at 88.[51]

Indeed, there are indications that this process of allocating loans and discounts on the basis of customer accounts may have been the bank's principal rationing mechanism. In August 1829 Roberts informed John T. Barr of Baltimore that the bank had experienced a particularly heavy demand for loans, "being altogether disproportionate to our income. We of course had to sponge," added Roberts, "which was done to the Amot. of from 50 to 75 percent and of the best notes of our City. We have many heavy a/c's in the Bk, the average balance of which are from $10–$20,000—these accounts we consider at least entitled to recieve their proportion of its loans, very frequently however during the Winter and Spring and now we find it difficult to apportion, owing to the accumulation of a/c's and . . . offerings."[52]

A detailed description of this credit-rationing process is continued in a letter to Arthur Tappan of New York in 1830. "It is our rule," said Roberts, "to exhibit each day the specie and average balance of each applicant's a/c and in proportion to the balance and the amount of business done M. G. apportions his loans and the accounts of many of them [are] large."[53] This description suggests that regular customers, or those dealing frequently with the bank, received favored treatment, pro-vided of course that their "account current" was of sufficient size.

The years 1829 and 1830 are particularly good examples of periods in which the interest rate or discount rate ceased to function as an effi-cient allocative mechanism. As table 14 indicates, short-term interest

Table 14

Average bank discount rate (sixty-day notes), 1812–1831

Date[a]		Average bank rate	Date		Average bank rate	Date		Average bank rate
1812	1	5.90	1819	1	5.45	1826	1	5.19
	2	5.60		2	5.35		2	5.46
	3	5.98		3	5.81		3	5.51
	4	5.94		4	5.63		4	5.67
1813	1	5.52	1820	1	5.43	1827	1	5.88
	2	5.74		2	5.54		2	5.47
	3	5.81		3	5.41		3	5.80
	4	5.84		4	5.24		4	5.43
1814	1	5.92	1821	1	5.07	1828	1	5.34
	2	5.93		2	5.43		2	5.23
	3	6.07		3	5.53		3	5.15
	4	6.28		4	5.43		4	5.00
1815	1	6.07	1822	1	5.55	1829	1	4.92
	2	6.15		2	5.60		2	5.47
	3	5.39		3	5.47		3	5.03
	4	5.50		4	5.59		4	5.90
1816	1	5.69	1823	1	5.40	1830	1	5.91
	2	5.84		2	5.64		2	6.06
	3	5.78		3	5.54		3	6.14
	4	5.75		4	5.63		4	6.02
1817	1	5.79	1824	1	5.37	1831	1	5.12
	2	5.36		2	5.84		2	5.95
	3	5.62		3	5.14		3	5.45
	4	5.85		4	5.97			
1818	1	5.42	1825	1	5.32			
	2	5.48		2	5.88			
	3	5.52		3	5.57			
	4	5.33		4	5.62			

Source: SGC, III, 1–16. Series is derived by averaging 100 sixty-day notes for the months of January, April, July, and October. Thus each year represents sample of 400 sixty-day notes, and the total sample for the entire period represents over 8,000 sixty-day notes.

a. Data are for January, April, July, and October of the years indicated.

rates at Girard's bank increased rapidly during this period, exceeding the legal limit of 6 percent by the summer of 1830.⁵⁴ In 1829 the loan/asset ratio reached a historic high of .540, and the ratio of loans to earning assets stood at .803. In short, the bank was strained to the point where interest rates could no longer allocate loanable funds among competing users. It is interesting to note that Girard's alternative credit-rationing schemes are among those commonly used by commercial banks today.

One method of handling temporary increases in the demand for credit—the overdraft system—was rejected by Girard. Under this practice, book credit was automatically extended to regular customers by allowing them to overdraw their accounts. This concept clashed with Girard's basic philosophy that businessmen should not extend themselves beyond their current means. For example, in February 1829 J. W. Zacharie was reminded that "in regard to prevailing on the Bank it is a rule with us not to pay drafts except the funds to meet them are in [the] Bk. at the credit of the drawer and in the subject particularly I must request you to make arrangements with Mr. Girard who is very particular and very strictly observes the same rule in his own private a/c."⁵⁵

An even harder tone was adopted with one John Boyer of Reading. He was told, "Your checks having been in several instances presented when you had no funds here oblige me to acquaint you that our rule is to close a/c's with those who overdraw—or attempt to overdraw the Bk. . . . I am obliged to decline receiving any future remittances of similar purposes."⁵⁶

Another rationing scheme available to Girard was the size of notes offered for discount. The fact that Girard apportioned the size of loans and discounts according to the size of borrowers' accounts does not imply that the bank preferred large borrowers, only that to obtain a large loan one needed a large account. In fact there is evidence, both qualitative and quantitative, to suggest that if loans were rationed on this basis, the preference was in favor of small borrowers. A contemporary observer noted that Girard's banking philosophy led him to discount "all the small notes that were considered good . . . in preference to those that were large." Girard sought to accomplish three objects by this system—"to accommodate small dealers, promote the industry of young beginners in trade, and to divide the risks for the security of the banker."⁵⁷ There is some evidence to indicate how successfully these goals were pursued.

An analysis of notes discounted at Girard's bank shows that there was little net change in the mean value between 1813 and 1822. However, following Simpson's death in the latter year, there was a significant decline in the average size of notes discounted. A summary of these changes indicates that (1) the mean value of notes discounted at Girard's bank was $1,498.21 in 1812, $1,456.75 in 1822, and $754.42 in 1831; and (2) the share of notes discounted in excess of $750.00 decreased over time, with the share of notes under $250.00 increasing by 208 percent. Thus if the trend toward discounting smaller notes was indicative of a large number of small borrowers, then Girard's customers may well have been changing.

A more likely explanation of the changing distribution of notes discounted was the desire to spread the risk of default over a large number of customers. If we compare the value of notes overdue and unpaid to total loan volume, we gain some feeling for the default rate over time. Table 15 indicates that the decrease in average loan size did not result in

Table 15

**Bills and notes due as a percentage of
total loans, 1815–1831**

Date	Percentage	Date	Percentage
1815	6.96	1824	6.53
1816	3.12	1825	5.41
1817	3.53	1826	6.33
1818	2.14	1827	6.88
1819	2.59	1828	5.01
1820	5.97	1829	4.85
1821	5.95	1830	4.78
1822	3.96	1831	4.39
1823	7.07		

Source: SGC, II, 393–94.

a significant decline in the proportion of bad debts. While this ratio declined rapidly from 1815 (when the first data are available) to the autumn of 1819, the subsequent financial panic sent rates to nearly 6 percent during 1820 and 1821. The ratio declined to prepanic levels in 1822, but 1823 witnessed an increase to an all-time high of over 7 percent. Between 1823 and 1831, the rate averaged 5.69 percent compared with a 4.27 percent average between 1815 and 1822.

From these data it would be easy to conclude that Girard's goal of reducing losses through the spreading of risk failed, but it is difficult to estimate what the losses would have been in the absence of such a policy. Over time Girard was probably required to discount notes with a somewhat higher risk factor because of the increasing number of banks in Philadelphia and the consequent increase in competition for short-term, local, commercial loans. Thus as time went on Girard was able to discount smaller notes but only at longer maturities.

Girard did not pay interest on deposits at his institution. He apparently regarded this practice as a matter of personal principle and considered it a point in favor of his bank. It was his contention that the integrity, safety, and reputation of his institution should be sufficient to attract depositors without his offering monetary rewards. In his memorial to the Senate and House of Representatives of the commonwealth of Pennsylvania in 1814, Girard proudly maintained that "there is not a single instance in which interest has been allowed to a company or to an individual even upon deposits, however great in amount or protracted in duration."[58] Girard's consistent opposition to interest payments may indicate that he preferred to specialize in demand deposits in his liability management, since his refusal to pay interest was not likely to attract time deposits. Quantitatively, "individual" deposits fluctuated between a quarter of a million and one-half million dollars in most years between 1812 and 1831. The most notable exception was 1824, when this category stood at $798,982.65 during the third quarter. The average number of depositors over the years was almost 380, although it exceeded 500 in 1820 and again in 1823. Most banks of the early nineteenth century did not distinguish between demand deposits and time deposits in their accounts. However, from May 1815 to July 1817, Girard's balance sheets list "Deposit Certificates" on the liability side. This account reached a maximum of $70,226.30 in April 1816, a sum equal to approximately 14 percent of individual deposits.[59] Over the entire period during which they appear, deposit certificates averaged a little over 5.5 percent of individual deposits. The deposits appeared to be for safe-keeping only. A typical receipt states that on 7 September 1814, "John Brown has this day deposited in this Bank for safe-keeping nine kegs marked JB no. 1-a9 said to contain five thousand dollars, to be held at the sole risk, and subject to the Order of said John Brown upon the receipt being returned."[60] Unfortunately it is not possible to determine whether the disappearance of this account on the balance sheets indicates its disappearance or absorption into the individual deposit accounts. The initial and terminal dates suggest that such deposits may have been a temporary phenomenon connected to the suspension of specie payments and the increased apprehension of owners of gold and silver.

To summarize Stephen Girard's Bank pursued policies reflecting the innate conservatism of its founder. As a proponent of the commercial-loan theory of banking, Girard did his utmost to insure that his portfolio of assets was made up largely of notes representing real commercial transactions. Ironically, while his own commercial contacts spanned the globe, Girard limited his bank's lending to residents of Philadelphia. Aggressive policies were not pursued to attract borrowers or depositors, and a policy of full specie reserves and the limited use of post notes indicated that Girard was as conservative with regard to the bank's issue as in the area of loans.

Girard eschewed the techniques and values of the new class of merchants and bankers who began to make their appearance following the War of 1812. In a rare expression of personal philosophy, Girard expressed his thoughts on this new species to John Stoney of Charleston in 1817. "Our city abounds," said Girard, "with that class of amateures who generally breakfast at 9 or 10 o'clock in the forenoon and immediately after are on the alert to borrow money or notes to pay or renew before 3 o'clock the notes which they have due in Bank, and [expend] the remainder of the day with what they call their friends in eating, drinking, smoking, talking of business which does not concern them and whenever some of their commercial operations prove disadvantageous which is often the case they attribute it to a bad luck and in view to make up the deficiency they have resources to a new accommodation which is discounted in Bank and renewed when in maturity or sold to some of our shavers."[61]

In contrast, Girard portrayed his own habits and those of his bank as proper, sound, and prudent, but at the same time fair. "So impartial is the accommodation of the bank," said Girard, "that every Citizen fairly entitled to Credit has found it there for a period of lending considerably beyond the usual period of discount . . . this is true whether he was a merchant, farmer, mechanic or manufacturer and whether [the] loan was for private or business use, or for the completion of Turnpike Roads and other Public works."[62] One is forced to wonder whether Jacob Barker, George Harrison, or other disappointed borrowers would have concurred with Girard's self-portrait.

7

Structure and Performance

In the pursuit of profits, banks differ little from other business ventures. Risk aversion, the protection of depositors, the desire to serve a particular class of customer, or the disposition to aid the state or the federal government in time of need were all secondary concerns compared to the principal touchstone of economic success—profit.

At Girard's bank, as at all commercial banks, the key profit-generating activities were asset management and liability management. The former involved choosing the appropriate balance of earning and nonearning assets, as well as the proper mix of income-producing financial paper. Liability management is a more subtle process that involves controlling the inflow and outflow of liabilities. One goal of liability management is to reduce the variation in the level of demand liabilities. By doing so, a commercial bank is able to safely support a larger volume of demand liabilities with a given supply of liquid, reserve assets.

We have already noted that Girard eschewed the most commonly utilized forms of liability management of the period, such as interest on demand deposits, the issue of post notes and small-denomination bank notes, and the circulation of notes in distant cities, to list only a few. Girard's operations were not, however, without liability management aspects. The requirement that prospective borrowers keep minimum balances at the bank was one attempt to reduce the variation in both deposits and bank notes. Girard's successful campaign to have his bank designated a federal depository was the basis of still another form of liability management, wherein the inflow of Treasury deposits would offset the reduction in other demand liabilities. This compensation re-

Table 16

Variability of bank notes and
demand deposits, expressed as
absolute percentage-change per quarter

Date	Bank notes	Demand deposits (individual)
1815	32.86%	16.42%
1816	19.87	16.41
1817	16.36	21.13
1818	7.99	24.40
1819	11.57	19.70
1820	5.51	18.37
1821	13.01	13.09
1822	9.36	12.66
1823	5.615	18.24
1824	9.69	29.17
1825	7.29	15.28
1826	6.45	24.92
1827	6.37	16.99
1828	5.21	23.33
1829	13.39	8.13
1830	15.61	13.37

Source: SGC, II, 393–94.

duced the pressure to sell off earning assets or reserve assets to meet the demands of depositors and noteholders.

Table 16 indicates the quarterly variation of both bank notes and demand deposits at Girard's bank between 1815 and 1830. These data, in isolation, are an inadequate basis for evaluating the success or failure of the bank's liability management efforts. Moreover, it is virtually impossible to compare these proportions to modern values. What the figures do indicate, however, is some tendency for the variability in banknote liabilities to decline after the first postwar years and the fact that the variability of demand deposits was nearly always greater than that of bank notes. This may indicate that to the extent that liability management was pursued, it was most effective in reducing the variability of that item which was directly related to the bank's primary reserve—specie.

More important to the over-all profitability of the bank was the management of its earning assets. Having insured the bank's safety through the provision of sufficient primary and secondary reserves, Girard was faced with the problem of selecting an asset portfolio that conformed to the special needs of his institution and at the same time generated the desired level of profits. This choice was complicated by such exogenous factors as changes in the demand for credit, changes in the supply of appropriate commercial and financial paper, and changes in both long- and short-term interest rates.

For purposes of classification, it is helpful to divide the bank's earn- ing assets into two broad categories—loans and investments. While the distinction between these is often blurred, loans can be defined as the acquisition of short-term debt instruments, and investment as the pur- chase of longer-term earning assets. Discounts, which are distinguished from loans only by the point at which interest is paid, are considered as part of the latter.

In the investment category, Girard quite clearly favored government stock and equity in the Bank of the United States. Since there was a ready market for such securities, they served another purpose as secondary reserves. Table 17 indicates that Girard clearly favored the obligations of the federal government over those of the states. However, when the availability of state bonds increased in the 1820s, those of the commonwealth of Pennsylvania began to appear in the bank's portfolio. For Girard, who valued integrity and soundness more than most, rela- tions with the often embarrassed state treasury in Harrisburg were not always harmonious. In 1829 the credit of the state was shaken by "improvident expenditures of the public money" on the internal-improve- ment system, and the governor was forced to call a special session of the legislature to deal with the problem. Faced with the state's imminent bankruptcy and the cessation of public-works projects, Girard stepped forward to lend $100,000 to the commonwealth. According to Simpson, this was "an act of public spirit to meet a great public exigency," rather than an ordinary investment.[1] Girard's public spirit did not hide his dis- appointment at the state's inability to repay the loan, however, and in a letter to the state treasurer on 31 December 1829 he noted, "I have just received your letter of the 30th inst. by [which] you propose to pay me on accot of the loan of $100,000 which I have made to the Common- wealth for canal and railroad purposes, the sum of $27,000. Altho it would be agreeable to me to receive the whole amot at once, yet as money is scarce, I accept your offer and will be much pleased to receive the remainder from time to time when it can be obtained."[2]

For a brief period in 1824, the bank held a small amount of New York State bonds, and between 1812 and 1820, some stock of the city of Philadelphia. Thus Girard appears to have successfully avoided the temptation to invest in the increasingly speculative issues of states seized by "canal fever" or otherwise preoccupied with various internal-improve- ment schemes. In this regard, Girard's unchartered status was helpful.

Table 17

Government stocks held by Stephen Girard's Bank, excluding stocks held in trust and as collateral

Date (1 Oct.)	U.S. 6%	U.S. 3%	Treasury notes	Pennsylvania 6%	New York 6%	Philadelphia 6%
1812	$ 65,574	$68,152	$ —	$ —	$ —	$45,200
1813	318,108	68,152	76,900	—	—	12,800
1814	1,245,227	68,152	76,900	—	—	4,400
1815[a]	1,431,276	62,453	88,093	—	—	4,000
1816	1,132,578	1,250	—	—	—	3,600
1817	1,016,882	1,250	—	—	—	3,200
1818	610,989	1,250	—	—	—	2,800
1819	489,822	1,250	—	—	—	2,400
1820	504,208	20,438	—	—	—	2,200
1821	504,208	20,438	—	—	—	—
1822	505,308	20,428	—	—	—	—
1823	531,801	20,438	—	—	—	—
1824	555,363	20,438	—	—	7,500	—
1825	578,240	20,438	—	—	—	—
1826	554,922	27,338	—	—	—	—
1827	559,823	51,691	—	2,000	—	—
1828	141,106	51,691	—	2,000	—	—
1829	53,907	51,691	—	2,396	—	—
1830	—	51,691	—	16,443	—	—
1831	—	51,691	—	16,443		

Source: SGC, II, 393–94.

a. 1 September.

The nature of the charters granted to many institutions required them to come to the aid of the state when conditions warranted, thus removing some flexibility in their portfolio decisions.

As for the bank's holdings of 6 percent stock, they consisted of three distinct issues. From the bank's beginning to 1816, Louisiana stock formed part of its assets, and after 1813 Girard added the stock he acquired in the loan of 15 April 1813. In early 1816, the bank acquired $100,000 in 6 percent stock of 1815 in return for $95,000 in Treasury notes as part of the Treasury's postwar refunding scheme. Holdings of 6 percent stock reached a peak in 1813 but declined rapidly throughout 1818. In the latter year, cash entries from the sale of 6 percents between 9 January and 16 September amounted to $407,231.24. Additional sales of $407,820.41 were recorded during 1828, and on 30 June 1830, Girard's remaining $53,906.62 in 6 percents was liquidated for cash.[3]

The substantial holdings of 3 percent stock that figured in the bank's initial capital declined sharply in 1816 to a level of only $1,250.00, where they remained until 1820. Purchases in 1820 and in 1826–1827 raised these holdings to $51,690.85 by 1831.

Treasury notes played only a brief role in the bank's portfolio of government obligations but were the subject of a very active episode of asset management by Girard. The bank first acquired these short-term obligations of the Treasury as part of the latter's attempt to raise wartime revenue. While they were redeemable within one year of issue, Girard, along with other bankers and individuals, was persuaded to renew or hold these notes beyond their date of maturity as an added favor to the Treasury. However, by early 1815 Girard was actively speculating in Treasury notes that were purchased in the South at varying rates of discount. The regional differences in price were largely due to the fact that Treasury notes were receivable in payment of debts owed to the federal government. Since the lion's share of these debts were incurred to the North, and since suspension of specie payments made coin hard to come by, the demand for notes in New York and Philadelphia was brisk and the price accordingly higher than in the South.

In January 1815 Girard's assets included substantial bank balances in Baltimore and Washington—$51,986 at the City Bank of Baltimore and $54,661 at the Bank of Washington—which, because of suspension, constituted idle balances. Thus Girard had Simpson order James Sterett, cashier of the City Bank of Baltimore, to purchase on Girard's account $30,000 in Treasury notes which he believed to be selling at a 4 percent discount there. Simpson also requested Sterett to keep him informed of price changes in these notes and the probability of his obtaining more if he wanted.[4] On 23 January, Sterett was ordered to increase Girard's purchases to $40,000, and Nathaniel Lewis was ordered to proceed to Washington to invest a draft of $50,000 in notes of Philadelphia, New York, or Trenton or drafts on banks in any of those places if they were available at par or a premium of not over 2.5 percent. The balance, if any, was to be invested in Treasury notes at the lowest price not exceeding par.[5] In February, John Heaton was dispatched on a similar mission to Washington and ordered to invest a $25,000 draft in Treasury notes at or under par and in drafts on New York, Boston, and Philadelphia banks at a 2.5 percent premium or less.[6] At the same time, Sterett in Baltimore was ordered to make an additional purchase of $20,000 in Treasury notes at or under par.[7]

Through these combined operations, Girard reduced his balances in

Baltimore and Washington to $8,967.05 and $1,074.93 respectively by 1 March 1815. At the same time, the bank's holdings of Treasury notes increased from $76,900.00 to $103,440.71.[8]

Later that same year Girard demonstrated how liability management and asset management could be combined to the bank's advantage. To assist the Treasury in paying its debts in the North, Girard had the Bank of South Carolina credit Treasury drafts payable in the South to his account in Charleston while he created an equivalent deposit for the Treasury in his bank in Philadelphia. Thus the Treasury could pay by drawing on this account at Girard's bank, and Girard could purchase depreciated Treasury notes with his Charleston funds.

Girard was not alone in these investments in government stock, and estimates indicate that federal and state debt made up almost 10 percent of the earning assets for the average bank during the early nineteenth century.[9] However, government stock seemed to play a larger role in Girard's portfolio than that of the average bank, particularly in the years during and immediately following the war. Some idea of the bank's importance in the government-bond market can be gained by considering the estimate that in 1815, "Seven out of the nine Philadelphia banks, including the Banking House of Stephen Girard, had invested $3,648,689 out of a capital of $7,734,000 in government stock, treasury notes, and corporation stock."[10] Thus Stephen Girard's bank held over 45 percent of the total stock held by the city's banking system. Girard was the largest holder of the public debt in the city, which itself held the largest share of any city in the nation. As table 18 indicates, Girard's holdings of the public debt declined over time. This decreasing importance cannot be entirely attributed to conscious asset management since the total federal debt was dwindling rapidly during the 1820s because of a series of Treasury surpluses and was entirely paid off by 1835.

Closely resembling the federal debt in terms of liquidity and safety were the shares of the Bank of the United States. Girard was a major stockholder in both the First and Second Banks of the United States and at some point was the largest individual shareholder in each. As table 19 illustrates, the bank's holdings of stock in the First BUS declined rapidly between 1812 and 1813, disappearing altogether in 1815.[11] Subscribing heavily to the shares of the Second BUS during the late summer of 1816, Girard increased the bank's holdings of these equities until they exceeded $726,000 by 1825.

Not only were BUS shares a steady source of income in the form of dividends, they also served a secondary reserve function. Indeed, the increasing importance of BUS shares in the bank's portfolio roughly parallels the decline of Treasury debt. Shares in the BUS formed an

Table 18

The public debt at
Stephen Girard's Bank

Date (1 October)	Total government debt	Government debt as percentage of total assets	Annual interest on government debt
1812	$ 178,925.89	6.81%	$ 4,784.96
1813[a]	290,848.83	5.85	2,204.19
1814	1,394,679.82	40.85	—
1815[b]	1,585,822.27	40.68	68,662.13
1816	1,137,427.61	23.86	99,297.75
1817	1,021,331.94	28.36	64,004.14
1818	615,038.65	16.31	46,377.26
1819	493,472.05	13.29	31,101.59
1820	524,646.49	13.92	31,055.00
1821	524,646,49	13.35	31,923.08
1822	525,746.49	13.05	31,923.08
1823	552,239.98	12.71	31,038.94
1824	583,301.06	11.73	31,338.90
1825	598,678.39	12.90	31,338.88
1826	582,260.38	11.85	31,246.89
1827	613,514.55	11.82	30,970.92
1828	194,796.62	3.80	14,200.64
1829	107,993.82	2.02	6,107.46
1830	68,133.49	1.23	2,879.23
1831	68,133.49	1.12	906.88

Source: SGC, III, 94, and II, 393–94.

a. 1 September.
b. 1 May.

important component of the bank's earning assets between 1816 and 1831 and averaged more than 12 percent of total assets. Based on dividend payments and holdings of BUS stock, the average return was 4.89 percent, ranging from a low of 1.63 percent in 1821 to over 6 percent in 1828–1831. For purposes of comparison, U.S. 3 percent stock of 1790 produced an average yield of 3.74 percent during the identical time period.

The final component of the bank's investment portfolio consisted of a variety of ventures in the areas of transportation and mining. Table 20 lists these investments, along with the dates initiated and the amounts invested. From the timing of these investment decisions, it is clear that during the last five years of the bank's existence, Girard was moving rapidly in the direction of diversifying its assets to include noncommer-

Table 19

**Bank of the United States stock and
dividends, Stephen Girard's Bank**

Date (1 October)	BUS stock	Percent of total assets	Dividends (annual)
1812	$113,760.00	4.33%	$ —
1813	18,960.00	—	—
1814	18,960.00	—	—
1815	—	—	—
1816	532,585.55	11.17	—
1817	300,000.00	8.33	—
1818	450,000.00	11.93	27,750
1819	450,000.00	12.12	11,250
1820	450,000.00	11.94	—
1821	450,000.00	11.45	7,350
1822	570,625.12	14.16	23,391
1823	570,625.12	13.14	27,980
1824	718,325.12	14.45	27,980
1825	726,725.12	15.66	29,379
1826	726,725.12	14.80	32,177
1827	570,625.12	10.99	33,576
1828	570,625.12	11.14	36,374
1829	655,319.21	12.28	40,918.50
1830	655,319.21	11.91	44,317
1831	655,319.21	10.81	44,317

Source: SGC, II, 393–94; and III, 94, #2, p. 100, and #3, p. 126.

cial, nongovernmental projects with relatively long gestation periods.

The Schuylkill Navigation Company was involved in various improvements of navigation along the waterway for which it was named, and the Ridge Turnpike Company's legacy, Ridge Avenue, still carries Philadelphians from the center city area to the northwest suburbs. Railroad investments were becoming increasingly popular with many banks, and both the Mount Carbon and the Danville and Pottsville were linked to the development of the anthracite coal resources of the Schuylkill Valley. Girard's land holdings in Northumberland County were purchased from the trustees of the First Bank of the United States and possessed both mineral and timber potential.[12] In total, the bank invested $513,613.92 in these projects, $473,613.92 in the years 1827–1831 alone. On the bank's final balance sheet in February 1832, these ventures amounted to $495,592.92, 10.41 percent of the institution's total assets. As such they represented the fastest-growing components of the bank's portfolio.

Table 20

Noncommercial investments of
Stephen Girard's Bank

Firm	Date	Amount invested
Ridge Turnpike Company	March 1813	$ 10,000.00
Schuylkill Navigation Company	January 1824	10,500.00
	April 1824	3,500.00
	July 1824	10,500.00
	October 1824	5,500.00
Coal lands in Erie	April 1826	581.90
	August 1826	100.00
Schuylkill Navigation Company	April 1827	197,500.00
	July 1827	33,350.00
Coal lands in Erie	April 1828	369.78
	April 1830	252.88
Coal lands in Mahoney	July 1830	30,419.92
	October 1830	2,240.46
Mount Carbon Railroad	October 1830	30,000.00
Coal lands in Mahoney	January 1831	1,578.06
Coal lands in Mahoney and Cattawisa	April 1831	444.98
	May 1831	80,959.25
	July 1831	11,092.56
	October 1831	36,093.56
	November 1831	4,630.57
Danville and Pottsville Railroad Company	May 1831	20,000.00

Table 21 summarizes the bank's investment portfolio between 1812 and 1831. The decline in the importance of government stock is clearly visible; however, it is significant that government debts as a share of total assets did not fall below the 10 percent estimated average for all banks until 1827. Government securities thus remained an important, if not dominant, factor in the bank's earning assets until the last four years of its existence. This change is not inconsistent with the nearly con-

Table 21

Investment portfolio of Stephen Girard's Bank, 1812–1831

Date (1 Oct.)	Government		BUS		Other		Investment/ total assets
	Percentage total assets	Percentage earning assets	Percentage total assets	Percentage earning assets	Percentage total assets	Percentage earning assets	
1812	6.81	22.73	4.33	14.41	—	—	11.14
1813	5.85	—	—	—	—	—	—
1814	40.85	67.69	—	—	—	—	—
1815	40.68	74.53	—	—	—	—	40.68
1816	23.86	45.16	11.17	21.14	—	—	35.03
1817	28.36	46.42	8.33	13.63	—	—	36.69
1818	16.31	26.20	11.93	19.17	—	—	28.24
1819	13.29	24.24	12.12	22.11	—	—	25.41
1820	13.92	30.15	11.94	25.87	—	—	25.86
1821	13.35	28.04	11.45	24.05	—	—	24.80
1822	13.05	19.62	14.16	21.29	—	—	27.21
1823	12.71	19.63	13.14	20.29	—	—	28.85
1824	11.73	19.30	14.45	23.77	—	—	26.18
1825	12.90	18.28	15.66	22.19	—	—	28.56
1826	11.85	17.75	14.80	22.17	—	—	26.65
1827	11.82	18.46	10.99	17.17	—	—	22.81
1828	3.80	5.22	11.14	15.32	5.19	7.14	20.13
1829	2.02	2.74	12.28	16.65	5.46	7.40	19.76
1830	1.23	1.76	11.91	17.08	5.18	7.43	18.32
1831	1.12	1.56	10.81	15.04	5.84	8.13	17.77

Source: SGC, II, 393–94.

tinuous decrease in yield and availability of long-term government bonds following 1815.[13]

Stock of the Second Bank of the United States remained a relatively stable component of the bank's total assets over the entire period, varying between 10 and 15 percent. These assets averaged nearly one-fifth (19.8 percent) of earning assets over time, exhibiting some tendency to decline after 1827. Other investments remained a minor component of both total assets and earning assets until the spring of 1827, when Girard invested nearly a quarter of a million dollars in the Schuylkill Navigation Company. From 1828 until the bank closed in 1831, these "other" investments constituted between 5 and 6 percent of total assets and from 7 to 8 percent of earning assets.

On the whole, investments declined substantially as a percentage of total assets, falling from a share of about two-fifths of the total at the end of the war to less than one-fifth during the last four years of the bank's existence. Low and declining yields on long-term debt instruments and the gradual disappearance of the federal debt shifted the emphasis to loans as the major component of earning assets.

It is worth noting at this point that American banks were forced to deal in a wider variety of credit instruments than European banks. There was the *acceptance,* which was theoretically based on a commercial transaction and was presumably self-liquidating. This instrument, also referred to as a draft or domestic bill of exchange, was the counterpart of the European real bill. The second popular type of business paper was the *advance.* An advance might also be used in commercial transactions but it was, in effect, a promissory note from buyer to seller, collateralled not by the goods involved in the transaction, but by the personal security of the market or drawer. Such an advance was generally further secured by two or three endorsers or by some other form of security, such as real estate, stocks, or bonds.[14]

Both kinds of commercial paper required the endorsement of at least two recognized merchants and were often referred to as "double name paper." Thus advances that were not based on commercial transactions and were properly endorsed were indistinguishable from commercially based advances.[15] The latter credit instrument came to be known as *accommodation paper.* These were normally three- or four-month loans that bore the virtual guarantee of a renewal when due. In reality such loans were medium- or long-term credit instruments and were used in many instances for capital development projects. Country banks in particular specialized in accommodation paper because of the credit needs of agriculturalists and the scarcity of good, strictly commercial paper in rural areas. City banks were not free from accommodation paper, despite the greater availability of acceptances, but early bank records, including those of the best documented institutions, do not give separate totals for loans on personal security and domestic bills of exchange, but include both under the general heading of loans and discounts. Early discussions of bank credit indicate that the promissory note was the usual form of business paper discounted by banks during the first quarter of the nineteenth century.[16]

One measure of the importance of accommodation loans in Philadelphia was the public's reaction to attempts to curtail them. In 1816 the Bank of North America, the Farmer's and Mechanic's Bank, and the Bank of Pennsylvania attempted to reduce their liabilities in anticipation of the approaching resumption of specie payments by discriminating against accommodation loans and eradicating what they considered a "pernicious abuse." For so doing they were violently attacked by Mathew Carey, who argued that a large portion of the community could not possibly "have access to banks in any other form."[17]

Girard's attitude toward accommodation paper was clear. Under normal conditions, he would have no part of such loans and concentrated instead on commercial acceptances or advances secured by two local signatures. This rigid attitude did not, however, preclude considerable flexibility in the bank's loan policy, for there were still the questions of how much lending, how long to lend, to whom to lend, and in what amounts to lend.

Table 22 compares the loan/asset ratio at Stephen Girard's Bank with that of the average Pennsylvania bank. In all years for which data are available, the proportion of loans to total assets at Girard's bank was lower than that of the average Pennsylvania bank despite a substantial increase in loans from less than one-fifth of total assets in 1812 to over one-half by 1831.

Girard was increasingly inclined to substitute short-term private debt for long-term public debt in the bank's portfolio of earning assets. Thus underlying the increasing loan/asset ratio was a change in the relative importance of loans and investments. As table 23 clearly reveals, the ratio of loans to investments, which stood at .51 in the first year after the war, had climbed to 5.02 by 1831. The only significant departure from the tendency for this ratio to increase was the period 1820–1821, when loan demand faltered in the wake of a financial panic and an abrupt decline in the price level.

Along with the increased relative importance of lending there occurred a change in the term structure of the loan portfolio. Table 24 illustrates this change by means of the calculated "liquidity interval." This value is derived by comparing the average monthly inflow of payments on loans

Table 22

Loan/asset ratios of Stephen Girard's Bank
and the average Pennsylvania bank

Date	Stephen Girard's Bank	Average Pennsylvania bank
1812	.189	—
1813	—	—
1814	.195	.767
1815	.139	.758
1816	.178	.750
1817	.244	.777
1818	.340	.821
1819	.294	.804
1820	.203	.743
1821	.228	.694
1822	.393	.725
1823	.389	.683
1824	.346	.689
1825	.420	.668
1826	.401	.670
1827	.412	.659
1828	.526	.598
1829	.540	.659
1830	.514	.611
1831	.541	.714
Average	.342	.711

Sources: SGC, II, 393–94, and Van Fenstermaker, *Development of American Commercial Banking*, p. 224.

to the average value of loans outstanding for each year between 1815 and 1831. The result is the average number of months required to repay the institution's entire stock of loans, which serves as a proxy for the average maturity of loans in force. Viewed in a slightly different fashion, the liquidity interval indicates how rapidly the banks can retrench in the face of a crisis. The data indicate a reasonably clear trend toward longer liquidity intervals, which in turn reflects the bank's increased willingness to accept notes with longer periods to run to maturity. Moreover, wherever qualitative data can be used to supplement these calculations, the calculated value for a given year is very near the maximum repayment period allowed on loans and discounts. For example, on 29 January 1824 the maximum maturity allowed by the bank was 100 days, and the liquidity interval for the year was 3.076, or 92.4 days.[18] When

Table 23
Loans, investments and total assets

Date	Loans		Investments		Loan/investment ratio	
	Percentage total assets	Percentage earning assets	Percentage total assets	Percentage earning assets	Stephen Girard's Bank	Average Pennsylvania bank
1812	18.9	62.86	11.14	37.14	1.69	—
1813	—	—	—	—	—	—
1814	19.5	—	—	—	—	—
1815	13.9	—	40.68	—	—	—
1816	17.8	33.70	35.03	66.30	.51	—
1817	24.4	39.95	36.69	60.05	.66	—
1818	34.0	54.63	28.24	45.37	1.20	—
1819	29.4	53.65	25.41	46.35	1.16	12.10
1820	20.3	43.98	25.86	56.02	.78	9.935
1821	22.8	47.91	24.80	52.09	.92	8.440
1822	39.3	59.09	27.21	40.91	1.44	7.982
1823	38.9	60.08	28.85	39.92	1.50	4.408
1824	34.6	56.93	26.18	43.07	1.32	6.526
1825	42.0	59.93	28.56	40.47	1.47	6.356
1826	40.1	60.08	26.65	39.92	1.50	5.226
1827	41.2	64.37	22.81	35.63	1.81	4.636
1828	52.6	79.46	20.13	20.54	3.87	2.740
1829	54.0	80.35	19.76	19.65	4.09	4.251
1830	51.4	81.16	18.32	18.84	4.31	4.216
1831	54.1	83.40	17.77	16.60	5.02	7.317

Source: See table 27 and SGC, II, 393–94.

Structure and Performance

Table 24

Liquidity interval of
Stephen Girard's Bank

Date	Liquidity interval	Date	Liquidity interval
1815	1.942	1824	3.076
1816	1.843	1825	3.165
1817	2.349	1826	3.032
1818	2.313	1827	3.989
1819	2.081	1828	3.801
1820	2.865	1829	4.331
1821	3.310	1830	4.699
1822	2.476	1831	5.025
1823	2.678		

Source: SGC, III, 94, #1, pp. 112–19, 228; #2, pp. 38–57, 404–5; #3, pp. 66–86; #4, pp. 56–75, 89; #5, p. 52.

the maximum was 120 days in 1828, the liquidity interval was 114 days.[19] When Girard reduced the maximum maturity from 180 days to 150 days in 1831, the liquidity interval for the entire year was 150.75 days.[20] Several explanations may account for this change. As the number of banks in Philadelphia grew, the competition for low-risk, short-term business paper increased, and Girard, along with the other institutions of the city, was compelled to accept longer-term notes. It is also probable that improvements in the efficiency of the capital market reduced the risk of holding longer-term paper.

Still another decision in managing the bank's loan portfolio involved the size of loans and discounts. There is no evidence that Girard maintained a maximum or minimum loan size, but there is evidence that the size distribution of loans changed over time. Table 25 exhibits the nature of that change. Loans under $500 increased dramatically, constituting 25.8 percent of total loans in 1812 and 53.6 percent in 1831. Over the same period, loans of less than $250 increased their share of the total nearly threefold. Loans in the $250–449 range increased from 18.4 percent of the total to 30.8 percent and comprised the largest single category of loans in 1812 and 1831.

At the other end of the spectrum, loans of over $1,500 declined as a share of the total, with those over $3,000 exhibiting the largest decline. Loans in the range of $500–749 were characterized by the most stable share over time, with those in the $750–999 and $1,000–1,499 category showing slight decreases. The clear tendency for smaller loans to predominate in the bank's portfolio as time wore on was reflected in the

Table 25

Distribution of notes discounted at
Stephen Girard's Bank,
1813–1831

Date	$0–249	$250–499	$500–749	$750–999	$1000–1499	$1500–1999	$2000–2999	$3000 and over	Average
1813	7.4	18.4	15.4	11.4	14.1	10.1	11.1	12.0	$1498.21
1814	8.0	13.9	10.7	13.9	11.7	13.9	17.6	10.0	1454.60
1815	8.5	18.1	14.3	9.5	20.0	12.4	15.2	1.9	1085.09
1816	4.9	22.1	17.7	11.6	15.1	9.3	10.1	8.9	1307.89
1817	8.6	21.6	13.9	11.4	18.5	7.7	12.3	5.4	1172.24
1818	7.3	23.5	16.4	12.3	16.1	7.0	10.3	6.6	1254.32
1819	10.1	28.0	16.2	12.6	12.2	8.1	9.5	2.8	1386.42
1820	19.2	28.0	18.9	12.3	10.4	3.9	5.2	1.9	1358.91
1821	25.1	25.1	19.3	11.1	8.2	2.9	5.8	2.4	1255.82
1822	17.1	29.1	17.1	14.3	10.6	4.6	4.6	2.1	1456.75
1823	20.4	33.8	20.1	9.6	9.3	3.0	1.6	1.8	634.85
1824	21.9	31.5	16.3	9.9	6.7	6.4	3.5	3.3	1116.64
1825	21.6	30.1	21.3	9.1	8.8	3.3	2.7	2.7	1075.59
1826	16.9	28.7	18.7	14.1	8.7	3.8	6.4	2.4	791.80
1827	27.3	29.3	11.5	8.0	9.4	5.7	4.8	3.6	765.79
1828	17.9	32.8	15.8	8.5	8.7	5.8	3.1	7.0	907.83
1829	15.9	30.5	18.6	10.8	10.1	6.2	4.6	3.0	803.51
1830	20.4	38.7	17.5	7.8	8.0	2.6	2.9	1.6	631.71
1831	22.8	30.8	16.3	8.1	10.9	3.5	4.4	2.7	754.42

Source: SGC, III, 1–6.

average size of loans. The year 1822 appears to be a turning point in this regard, and loan size, which never fell below $1,000 in the period 1812–1822, rose above $1,000 in only two years between 1823 and 1831.

Thus simultaneously with the trend toward longer loan maturities there was a clear tendency for average note size to decline. These two sets of changes no doubt reflect basic changes in the structure of the Philadelphia credit market and a change in the clientele of the Girard bank. Girard's policy of requiring borrowers to be depositors as well permits us to make an inference about the former group by an analysis of the bank's deposit structure. Table 26 indicates that little change took place in the distribution of individual deposits over itme. This lack of

Table 26

Distribution of individual deposits at
Stephen Girard's Bank, 1812–1831

Date (1 Jan.)	Average deposit	$0–99	$100– 499	$500– 999	$1000– 1999	$2000 and over
1812[a]	$1,431	33.2%	30.1%	12.3%	11.1%	10.4%
1813	1,147	34.2	31.6	11.2	10.3	11.2
1814	—	—	—	—	—	—
1815[b]	1,294	54.2	22.1	9.3	4.2	9.9
1816	1,391	49.6	21.0	10.1	7.1	11.2
1817	698	46.9	24.5	8.3	9.1	11.2
1818	949	55.2	22.8	8.1	6.8	7.2
1819	877	36.2	30.3	14.2	8.3	9.3
1820	556	41.5	30.2	12.1	8.2	6.5
1821	895	39.2	29.2	13.2	9.4	8.4
1822	795	39.3	26.1	11.2	13.3	8.3
1823	855	45.4	30.2	12.1	7.1	4.3
1824	1,080	42.4	32.8	9.3	9.3	6.3
1825	922	41.4	32.8	11.1	7.3	6.4
1826	767	44.4	25.3	11.3	8.4	8.8
1827	1,318	43.3	27.9	12.2	7.2	8.4
1828	1,291	37.4	29.5	14.2	9.2	9.2
1829	944	48.3	25.2	10.1	10.0	6.2
1830	929	43.3	30.3	12.8	6.2	6.1
1831	1,123	42.4	29.2	9.2	9.8	9.3

Source: SGC, II, 393–94.

a. 1 October.
b. 1 March.

Table 27

Occupations of depositors at
Stephen Girard's Bank,
1812 and 1832

Occupational category	1812	1832
General mercantile	34%	22%
Professional	11	13
Craftsman	15	9
Specialized mercantile	6	20
Financial	2.5	4
Gentleman or gentlewoman	1.5	10
Unknown	30	22
	100.0	100.0

Sources: SGC, II, 394.

significant change, however, conceals the fact that the bank's depositors (borrowers) were a more diverse group of individuals. With the assistance of the bank's records, it is possible to construct a rough profile of its customers in 1812 and at the closing of its affairs in 1832. Table 27 indicates that in occupational terms, the group that registered the greatest gain was the specialized mercantile category, while general mercantile customers declined from about one-third of the total to less than one-fourth. The latter group comprised large auctioneers and wholesalers, while the former were small, single-product retailers.

The over-all picture of change that results from this variety of data is consistent. As time passed, Girard moved to bring the distribution of loans into line with the distribution of deposits. This was particularly true following the death of George Simpson in 1822. The consequent decline in average loan size and the over-all greater importance of smaller notes in the bank's portfolio were accompanied by a change in the make-up of the bank's customers. These changes took place while the average maturity of both loans and discounts was increasing.

The success of Girard's portfolio decisions was to be measured in his bank's profits. Utilizing the most common measure of bank profitability—return on capital—it is possible to muster the appropriate data from the Girard records. The sources of revenue or income for early nineteenth-century banks were varied. There were, of course, the familiar items such as discounts or interest on loans, dividends on stock, and interest on the public debt. In addition, however, were categories such as "gain on gold," representing the premium paid to Girard by other banks or individuals for specie. In common with others, Girard was compelled to pay a premium for specie during and immediately after the period of general suspension, but by 1820 he was selling gold coins, often at a handsome profit. In 1820 and 1821, for instance, the sale of Spanish doubloons, half crowns, guineas, ducats, and uncoined specie brought premiums of 1 to 6.25 percent.[21] Likewise, revenue resulted from the sale of drafts on other banks in cities where funds were needed to meet obligations. For example, between January and April 1823, Girard sold drafts on Charleston for a premium and by the summer and fall of 1824 had expanded such sales to include drafts on New York and Boston. By the middle of 1828, drafts on Boston were commanding a premium of from .25 to .5 percent of the face value.[22] Collecting drafts on notes for other banks also produced income, and the standard charge for such operations was .5 percent of the face value.[23] Stock sales netted .25 percent commission, and Girard and other bankers often performed the role of note brokers, purchasing depreciated notes and selling or exchanging them at a profit.

Mint operations provided an additional source of income at Girard's bank. Customers who possessed specie in uncoined form (for example, plate or ingots) and who were in need of immediate cash advances could deliver the metal to Girard, who would forward it to the mint, where coinage would take from one to three months. Girard would then discount the mint receipt, providing the customer with needed cash.[24] Not only did Girard profit from discounting the mint receipt, but he was also free to sell the latter at a premium.

It is important to note that most of the above sources of revenue had their counterpart on the cost side, and Girard was often forced to pay the same premiums and commissions. In addition, as a banker, he was susceptible to losses through counterfeit notes and altered or forged checks.

As a first step in estimating the profits of Stephen Girard's Bank, table 28 details the major sources of revenue in the years for which sufficient data are available. From the outset and throughout the years in question, income from discounts and loans was the single most important source of revenue. Surprisingly, this was true even during the war years, when Girard's holdings of government stock were large and growing. As loans and discounts grew relative to other assets, so too did the income they generated. The years also saw an increase in dividends from BUS shares and a decline in revenue attributable to the public debt.

To estimate the gross profits of the bank, gross revenues (discount,

Table 28

Chief sources of operating revenue at
Stephen Girard's Bank,
1812–1831

Date	Discount[a]	Interest	Dividends on BUS stock	Interest on public debt
1812	$ 2,190.83	$ 1,362.00	$ —	$ 4,784.96
1813	67,479.56	18,351.46	—	2,204.19
1814	54,294.63	60,999.45	—	—
1815	11,244.91	75,180.07	—	68,662.13
1816	—	147,060.70	—	99,297.75
1817	—	142,270.03	—	64,004.14
1818	—	121,898.65	27,750.00	46,377.26
1819	—	111,924.86	11,250.00	31,101.59
1820	—	96,505.39	—	31,055.00
1821	—	86,408.73	7,350.00	31,923.08
1822	—	104,217.83	23,391.00	31,923.08
1823	—	131,776.98	27,980.00	31,038.94
1824	—	138,534.05	27,980.00	31,338.90
1825	—	151,032.79	29,379.00	31,338.88
1826	—	161,046.81	32,177.00	31,246.89
1827	—	167,169.03	33,576.00	30,970.92
1828	—	183,484.42	36,374.00	14,200.64
1829	—	206,518.28	40,918.50	6,107.46
1830	—	215,649.92	44,317.00	2,879.23
1831	—	207,193.30	44,317.00	906.88

Sources: Discount and interest, SGC, III, 94, #1, pp. 50–56, 59; #2, pp. 114–15; #3, pp. 88–96; #4, pp. 80–88, #5, pp. 76–85.

Dividends on BUS stock, SGC, III, 94, #2, p. 100; #3, p. 126; #4, p. 117.

Interest on Public Debt, see sources for discount and interest.

a. Discount ends on 4 March 1815.

dividend, and interest income) were compared with capital stock. This series, which appears in table 29 is only an approximation, since minor sources of revenue such as premiums and commissions, have been omitted. A more accurate calculation is the series labeled "net profit." This calculation utilized "income to profit and loss" as the revenue component and includes all sources of revenue and expenses as well. Net profits are thus defined as net income to profit and loss, divided

Table 29

Profits of Stephen Girard's
Bank, 1813–1830

Date	Net profit	Gross profit	Date	Net profit	Gross profit
1813	—	5.87	1823	3.68	7.63
1814	4.53	7.69	1824	10.31	7.91
1815	7.02	8.61	1825	3.84	8.47
1816	4.96	13.69	1826	7.85	8.98
1817	7.74	11.36	1827	6.82	7.72
1818	9.18	10.80	1828	7.25	7.80
1819	3.16	8.50	1829	8.35	8.45
1820	5.78	7.03	1830	8.74	8.76
1821	2.68	6.92			
1822	5.24	6.38			

Sources: SGC, III, 94, #1, p. 80, 149; #2, p. 73, 94; #3, pp. 112–14, 114–17; #4, pp. 102–7; #5, p. 96; SGC, III, 94, #1, pp. 50–56, 59; #2, pp. 114–15; #3, pp. 88–96; #4, pp. 80–88; #5, pp. 76–85. SGC, III, 94, #2, p. 100; #3, p. 126; #4, p. 117.

by capital stock. The absence of a consistent relationship between gross and net profits is due to variation in expenses over time, as well as to the changing relative importance of minor sources of income.

Fortunately, it is possible to compare the net profit data for Girard's bank with the same data for two contemporary institutions. As table 30 indicates, the dividends as a percentage of capital stock for both the Philadelphia Bank and the Massachussets Bank of Boston showed less fluctuation than the Girard data. On the other hand, the chartered institutions were under pressure from their stockholders to produce "acceptable" dividends. Dividends as a percentage of capital stock for the Philadelphia Bank averaged 5.40 percent between 1811 and 1831, while the same figure for the Massachussets Bank was 5.54 percent. Net profits as a percentage of capital stock at Stephen Girard's Bank averaged 6.42 percent between 1814 and 1831. Girard's best years were better than any years for the other institutions, and in the worst years his profits roughly equaled theirs. Profits rose above 8 percent in 1818, 1824, and 1829–1831 and fell below 3 percent in 1821. As a final comparative note, a study of some fourteen banking institutions in the early nineteenth century found that the average annual rate of dividends from their beginnings to 1830 was 5.5 percent.[25]

Outside of the banking field, comparative data become scarce. However, it is estimated that in 1835 dividends as a percentage of equity

Table 30

Profitability of the Philadelphia Bank,
the Massachusetts Bank of Boston, and
Stephen Girard's Bank,
1811–1831

Date	Philadelphia Bank[a]	Massachusetts Bank of Boston[a]	Stephen Girard's Bank[b]
1811	4.0%	8.0%	— %
1812	6.5	7.5	—
1813	8.0	4.75	—
1814	7.5	6.0	4.53
1815	7.5	3.0	7.02
1816	7.0	6.0	4.96
1817	7.0	6.0	7.74
1818	6.0	6.0	9.18
1819	3.0	6.0	3.16
1820	3.0	4.85	5.78
1821	4.0	6.0	2.68
1822	5.0	6.2	5.24
1823	5.0	6.0	3.68
1824	5.0	6.0	10.31
1825	5.0	6.0	3.84
1826	5.0	6.0	7.85
1827	5.0	3.7	6.82
1828	4.5	4.5	7.25
1829	5.0	4.5	8.35
1830	5.0	4.5	8.74
1831	5.5	4.9	8.45

Sources: Philadelphia Bank, Nicholas Wainwright, *The Philadelphia National Bank, 1803–1953* (Philadelphia, 1953), pp. 244–45.

Massachusetts Bank of Boston, Joseph Martin, *A Century of Finance* (New York, 1969), p. 97.

a. Dividends as a percentage of capital stock.
b. Net profits as a percentage of capital stock.

capital for mining corporations averaged 4 percent, and dividends as a percentage of capital stock for private canal companies were 3.1 percent. Gaslight companies in the same year paid dividends of about 4.7 percent as a percentage of paid-in capital.[26]

Girard appears to have done as well as or better than other banks of the period and considerably better than non-bank alternatives. Girard's success in this respect is all the more remarkable in view of the opposition his institution received from the state legislature and his Philadelphia competitors. Moreover, the bank prospered despite the wartime disruption of capital markets, the Panic of 1819, and the general suspension of specie payments. Through its founder's shrewdness and caution, his tenacity of character and excellent grasp of business and financial techniques, Girard's banking house grew and prospered in the face of adversity and good fortune alike.

8

A Final Accounting

Unlike its corporate counterparts, Stephen Girard's Bank was as mortal as its founder. On 27 December 1831 Joseph Roberts addressed a letter to eight other cashiers. "It has become my painful duty," he said, "to announce to you the death of our inestimable friend Mr. Girard who died yesterday afternoon about 4 o'clock."[1]

In December of the previous year, the old banker, then aged eighty, was struck by a wagon in the street, receiving a severe head injury. Exhibiting his characteristic tenacity, Girard managed to return to full-time duties at his bank by the summer of 1831. However, a respiratory disorder seized him in the late autumn of the same year. Complications ensued, and at last both body and spirit succumbed the day after Christmas, 1831.

At the time of his death, his institution possessed assets of over $6 million, and loans outstanding amounted to $3,200,797.76. There was in addition over $500,000 in individual accounts to be settled, as well as accounts current with a score of other banks in Philadelphia and elsewhere. Girard, of course, had anticipated this day, and the trustees moved swiftly to settle the affairs of the bank. Roberts advised George Newbold of the Bank of America that "the concerns of the Bank are to be closed as speedily as practical consistent with the interests and convenience of its customers and no further deposits can be received nor discounts made."[2] The same day Roberts informed J. T. Barr of Baltimore that "the Trustees meet twice a week on Wednesday, Saturdays when all propositions and communications which may be made will be laid before them."[3]

By 5 January 1832, notices of Girard's death had been prepared for insertion in the leading newspapers of the major cities, and on 9 January the first of Girard's correspondent banks moved to close out its account. William Paxson, cashier of the Bank of Delaware in Wilmington, contacted Roberts, enclosing a check "on the Bank of the United States draw to thy order for Six hundred thirty nine 64/100 dollars due by our books to the late Stephen Girard Banker."[4] Paxson further requested Roberts to acknowledge this payment and "say whether the amount is in full as due from this institution." The next day Roberts replied with an air of finality that "this is the balance of your Acco^t, and of course closes your transactions with this institution."[5] The 10 January mail brought more letters regarding final settlements from R. Michle, cashier of the Union Bank of Maryland in Baltimore, Samuel Payson, cashier of the Massachusetts Bank of Boston, and Thomas Poultney of Evan Poultney's Bank in Baltimore.

By mid-January rumors were abroad regarding the future intentions of the trustees. On 13 January Newbold informed Roberts that "the President of one of our most respectable City Banks having heard that the Trustees of your Bank have determined to loan to other Banks for a limited and specific time a portion of the funds of your institution at a reduced rate of interest has requested me to enquire of you whether such is the fact and if so whether you would make a loan to the Bank of which he is President, what sum, what time and at what rate of interest—the Bank that has requested me to make the enquiry is one of our oldest most substantive and respectable institutions."[6]

Roberts' reply was noncommittal. He told Newbold on the fourteenth that he had that very day laid his letter before the trustees, and "altho temporary arrangements for the accommodation of the customers of the Bank had been made with some of the Banks of the City, the Trustees do not intend making any permanent loans of the money and will add that it is not, I believe contemplated by any of the Trustees to make any loans whatever out of this City and—liberties."[7]

In fact, the trustees lent large sums of the bank's assets at a rate of 4 percent to several local banks. The trustees entered this arrangement with considerable caution. On 16 January Roberts was directed to inform the Penn Township Bank, the Bank of Northern Liberties, the Southwark Bank, the Commercial Bank, the Mechanic's Bank, and others of the acceptance of their proposal to settle affairs. However, Roberts pointed out, "it is expressly understood that the terms mentioned in the said proposals on which the deposits will be made are not altered: but that the Trustees reserve to themselves the entire right to regulate and control the balance which may become due from all or any of the said Banks."[8]

Out-of-town banks were now called upon to settle their accounts as quickly as possible, and a correspondent of long standing, the Farmer's Bank of Lancaster, terminated nearly twenty years of close association with a curt note stating that "your account is credited $430 for a package of notes delivered by Mr. Mayer."[9] John Stoney, Girard's friend and confidant in Charleston, made sufficient deposits to cover his notes and closed out his account of $10,636 on 2 February 1831.[10]

The Massachusetts Bank of Boston inquired about a new Philadelphia correspondent, requesting the name of the safest institution that did not have a correspondent in Boston so that the relationship could be reciprocal "and collections of one . . . be placed against those of the other."[11] Roberts recommended the Bank of North America, which was, he said, "in point of solidity and correct management I believe behind none of our Banks."[12]

Banks were requested to settle accounts immediately, and for those which did not the trustees provided an incentive in the form of a graduated penalty. In one instance, the trustees agreed to the extension of four notes, "5 percent being paid on the first two renewals and 10 percent each renewal after, until all paid on each renewal at 60 days."[13]

The trustees had been pondering things other than the closing out of the bank's affairs. Their decision to apply for a charter and continue the Girard bank, at least in name, was soon the subject of rumor within financial circles. Newbold told Roberts that it was his understanding that a new bank was to be established in Philadelphia and added, "taking it for granted that you will be either its President or Cashier, I please myself with the hope that we may renew the intercourse and correspondence which has so long subsisted between us and that we may do the business of that Bank in this City."[14] Roberts replied that in truth three new institutions were contemplated in Philadelphia. "The Girard Bank," he said, "the one I presume you allude to, is chartered with a capital of $1,500,000, the other two it is expected will be—With respect to any appointment of myself in either of them, it is not my intention to accept of any. . . . To speak of answering the intercourse and correspondence which has so long subsisted between us awakens pleasurable feelings in my mind and will always be remembered by me with pleasure— But my dear Sir I do not intend to have anything to do with Banks except probably keeping a small amount in one after I have done with this—"[15]

Roberts underscored these intentions in a letter to Thomas Bacot, cashier of the Bank of South Carolina in Charleston. "The concerns of this Bank are rapidly progressing to a close," he noted, "and on its close it is my intention and long has been, if I should survive Mr. Girard, to close my business concerns, as far as practicable, *at least with Banks,* after thirty-six years which I have been in close confinement, without any time for relaxation, *not one day,* you may suppose that I both in Body & Mind require it and with pleasurable feelings, I anticipate a change—"[16]

Robert's long-awaited retirement was soon at hand as the bank's affairs wound down. A committee of the trustees counted the cash in the bank as of 26 December 1831 and found some $796,640.08 in specie and bank notes. Much of this was loaned to local banks pending its assignment to the executors of Girard's estate. The same committee also canceled and packed in boxes $837,410.00 of the bank's own notes which were slated for destruction.[17] The committee reported that there was in the vault:

$251,440	in $5 notes
207,350	in $10 notes
38,120	in $20 notes
79,000	in $50 notes
120,900	in $100 notes
48,500	in $500 notes
48,000	in $1,000 notes
39,800	in past notes

As for other assets, lending was immediately discontinued on Girard's death, and as repayments flowed, in the balances outstanding were quickly reduced.

On 1 January 1832, $3,226,356.70 in loans was outstanding. In subsequent months the same balance stood at:

$2,612,240.06	in February
1,771,364.67	in March
762,875.63	in April
180,459.47	in May

By 1 January 1833 the balance was $7,939.88. Some loans, of course were never collected, while others were granted renewals. In 1837, $1,777.49 in unpaid loans was turned over to the Girard estate.[18]

In the same year (3 January 1837), $162,864.23 in interest income was credited to the capital stock of the late Bank of Stephen Girard for disposition by the executors. The balance of the surplus fund, amounting to $1,208,083.48, was credited to capital stock on 7 March 1832, and $183,457.82 was credited to profit and loss. Thus on 6 January 1837 the capital stock account of the bank was $4,187,489.89.[19]

Girard's holdings of 6,331 shares of the Bank of the United States valued at slightly over 103.5 amounted to $655,319.21, and this was turned over to the executors of Stephen Girard on 11 January 1833.[20] In February 1834 another $172,474.06 was credited to the Girard estate by the trustees of the bank. This sum, labeled "not allowed by the court," evidently represented part of the trustees' commission.[21] In this fashion the remnants of Stephen Girard's Bank were slowly absorbed by the huge estate that was his final legacy.

In the summer of 1832, George Newbold (elected president of the Bank of America in May) was still soliciting the business of the new Girard Bank. He told Roberts that "if the new Bank in your City called the Girard Bank shall be respectably established, we shall be pleased to have their account & collect for them here, will you do me the favor to inform me respecting it and give me the names of the President and Cashier and if you shall think that the Bank will be well conducted, I shall feel obliged by any aid that you may render me in endeavoring to obtain this account."[22]

Roberts was obliged to report that all was not well with the newly chartered institution. "The Girard Bank is not yet organized," he wrote on 9 June. "The Board, etc. not yet formed, it is impossible to speak of its character at present, much discontent exists on Accot. of the manner in which the subscriptions were received."[23]

By late July 1832, Roberts, under orders from the trustees, began his final duty as cashier—calling in the loans to local banks. On 25 July, J. B. Mitchell of the Mechanic's Bank and Jacob Frick, cashier of the Bank of Penn Township, were informed that each institution owed $50,000, which would be collected one month hence on 24 August.[24] To William Patton, Jr., Roberts wrote on 1 August, that he had been directed "to notify the Farmer's and Mechanic's Bank that they will be called on at the expiration of thirty days from the date of the notice for One Hundred thousand dollars."[25] By year's end other borrowers were called for the balance of their debts. The Bank of North America was required to pay $50,000 within thirty days of January 1833 and $50,000 each succeeding thirty days until the entire sum had been paid.[26] The same day the Southwark Bank was instructed to repay $100,000 thirty days from 1 January 1833 and $100,000 each succeeding thirty days thereafter.[27]

The affairs of the bank dragged on, and the letter books of the bank do not end until 18 September 1835. By the time the books were closed on Stephen Girard's Bank, the newly chartered Girard Bank was well established. Ironically, the latter institution had become a pet bank of the Jackson administration and served as a depository for federal funds in lieu of the Second Bank of the United States. Thus the name of Girard became associated with both the birth and the death of the last "national bank."

The Bank of Stephen Girard was significant in many respects. In some ways the institution was unique, while in others it was representative of the changes that were taking place in banking systems as a whole. Many scholars have pointed to a shift in the flow of American capital during the early nineteenth century. The repeated interruptions of international commerce during the Embargo, Nonintercourse, and wartime years, so the story goes, prompted men of commercial wealth to focus their attention on domestic growth and development and divert their investments accordingly. Girard is a prime example of such a transition. His decision to withdraw a substantial portion of his active capital from foreign trade and establish a bank for the discount of domestic bills conforms to that pattern. During the last years of the bank, moreover, Girard was shifting the emphasis of the institution's lending activities more and more toward the area of internal improvements.

From its very inception the bank was heavily involved in Treasury financing. The wartime needs of the government drew the nation's commercial banks into an unprecedentedly close alliance with the fiscal authorities, an alliance that marked a permanent change in the Treasury's financing operations. Girard's bank played a special role in the area of federal finances by acting as the prime mover in the formation of the nation's first real investment syndicate. This group, headed by Girard, John Jacob Astor, and David Parish, set the tone for subsequent syndicate operations by introducing a system of pooled purchases of government bonds on the one hand and subcontracted sales on the other.

In the course of its day-to-day operations, Girard's bank also served a central reserve function for rural banks such as the Farmer's Bank of Lancaster and the Farmer's Bank of Reading. In return for keeping accounts at his Philadelphia institution, Girard accepted the notes of these institutions for deposit or exchange and thus permitted them to circulate in the city at par.

Perhaps the most characteristically unique facet of Girard and his bank was his resistance to the increasingly corporate nature of commercial banking. Girard was strongly opposed to the notion that individuals could constitutionally be prohibited from engaging in activities reserved to firms with corporate charters. He fought unsuccessfully against the Pennsylvania banking act of 1814, which limited the activities of unincorporated institutions, "because the power of Government relative to corporations, affords no analogy to justify as interference with the industrious and honest pursuits of an individual citizen, whose rights and priviledges [*sic*] flow from a constitutional source, equally independent of legislative control and patronage."

Girard was at the same time a link with the past and a precursor of things to come in the financial world. As a product of the eighteenth century, he exhibited many characteristics of his mercantilist past. However, as a financier of great influence, wealth, and flexibility, he foreshadowed the great investment bankers who were to dominate the latter half of the nineteenth century. Perhaps it is in this role as a bridge between the commercially oriented past and the dynamic era of domestic growth that Girard should be remembered.

Notes

Chapter 1

1. J. Van Fenstermaker, *The Development of American Commercial Banking, 1782–1837* (Kent, Ohio, 1965), p. 111, table A-1.

2. Fritz Redlich, *The Molding of American Banking: Men and Ideas* (New York, 1968), p. 7.

3. Bray, Hammond, "Long and Short Term Credit in Early American Banking," *Quarterly Journal of Economics* 49(1935):79.

4. Ibid., p. 93.

5. Redlich, *Molding of American Banking*, p. 8.

6. Ibid., p. 25.

7. Attributed to Mathew Carey in Redlich, *Molding of American Banking*, p. 9.

8. Bray Hammond, *Banks and Politics in America from the Revolution to the Civil War* (Princeton, 1957), p. 130.

9. Ibid.

10. Ibid., p. 135; also see John T. Holdsworth, *Financing an Empire: History of Banking in Pennsylvania* (Chicago, 1928):97–98, and *American State Papers,* Finance, 2:470.

11. Redlich, *Molding of American Banking,* p. 23.

12. Hammond, *Banks and Politics,* p. 193.

13. N. S. B. Gras, *The Massachusetts First National Bank of Boston: 1784–1934* (Cambridge, 1937), p. 7.

14. Stephen Girard Collection, Series III, Reel Number 125, Letter #13, (25 August 1815). Hereafter cited as SGC, III, 125, #13 (25 August 1815).

Chapter 2

1. For Girard's early life see: Stephen Simpson, *Biography of Stephen Girard* (Philadelphia, 1832), the only contemporary biography, written by the son of George Simpson, Girard's first cashier; H. E. Ingram, *The Life and Character of Stephen Girard* (Philadelphia, 1884); J. B. McMaster, *The Life and Times of Stephen Girard,* 2 vols. (Philadelphia, 1918), the most scholarly biography but written almost entirely from correspondence; Harry Emerson Wildes, *Lonely Midas* (New York, 1943), written in a more popular vein but nonetheless well researched and comprehensive.

2. Kenneth Brown, "Stephen Girard's Bank," *The Pennsylvania Magazine of History and Biography* 66 (1942): 30.

3. SGC, III, 125, #21 (31 October 1807).

4. Girard's conviction that his funds would be safe in London may indicate a belief that war with France was likely.

5. SGC, III, 125, #62 (26 December 1807).

6. SGC, III, 125 #77 (4 January 1808). In all conversions, the Pennsylvania pound (currency) is valued at $2.66. Thus an exchange rate of 175 for sterling translates to $4.655.

7. Ibid., #172 (5 April 1808).

8. Ibid., #173 (5 April 1808).

9. Ibid., #186 (3 May 1808).

10. Ibid., #288 (24 June 1808).

11. This would seem to indicate that bills on London had already achieved something of the status of an international medium of exchange.

12. SGC, III, 125, #215 (July 1808).

13. Ibid., #255 (3 October 1808).

14. Ibid., #263 (6 December 1808).

15. Ibid., #296 (7 February 1809).

16. Ibid., #297 (14 February 1809).

17. Ibid., #335 (25 May 1809).

18. Ibid., #380 (18 September 1809).

19. Ibid., #400 (2 November 1809).

20. Erskine was the British minister to the United States who worked out an agreement with Madison to rescind the Orders in Council against neutral shipping so that the United States could resume normal commercial activity with Britain. However, Canning, the foreign secretary, repudiated the agreement.

21. SGC, III, 125, #397 (3 November 1809).

22. SGC, III, 125, #96, and *American State Papers,* Finance, 2:641.

23. SGC, III, 125, #96 (May 1810).

24. Madison, falling into Napoleon's carefully laid trap, suspended trade with Britain in March of 1811 on the basis of the latter's promise to respect American neutrality.

25. Gallatin, the secretary of the treasury, had made it quite clear as early as 1809 that a war would be financed by borrowing.

26. Girard served on a committee of five which in 1810 drew up a memorial from Philadelphia in favor of rechartering the BUS.

27. *American State Papers,* Finance, 2:641, (9 March 1812).

28. SGC, III, 125, #211 (23 February 1811).

29. Only three days before, the Senate had defeated a recharter bill by one vote, with Vice President Clinton casting the decisive ballot.

30. SGC, III, 125, #260 (22 May 1811).

31. Ibid., #266 (5 June 1811).

32. Ibid. It is difficult to determine whether Girard was referring to a purely private activity here or if he had already decided to enter the commercial banking field.

33. SGC, III, 125, #99 (25 May 1810).

34. *American State Papers,* Finance, 2:641 (9 March 1812).

35. SGC, III, 125, #358 (23 December 1811).

36. Ibid., #377 (9 January 1812).

37. *American State Papers,* Finance, 2:641 (9 March 1812).

38. The cargo was shipped aboard the *Good Friends,* Robert Thompson, Master. Sailing from Portsmouth on 4 January 1812 with Charles Bancker, she arrived at Amelia Island, near the mouth of the St. Mary's River on 9 February. As a Spanish possession, Amelia Island was a haven for American bottoms waiting for suspension of nonintercourse. Unfortunately for Girard, American troops seized the island shortly before the arrival of the *Good Friends,* making her technically in violation of the law. Letters to James Monroe, the secretary of state, a memorial to Congress on 9 March 1812, and vigorous lobbying by friends and associates finally freed the *Good Friends* to land in Philadelphia. Girard was eventually forced to pay double duties on her cargo but still netted a handsome profit from its sale. A major share of this profit was capitalized in Stephen Girard's Bank.

39. SGC, III, 125, #383 (23 January 1812).

40. Ibid., #384 (23 January 1812).

41. Ibid., #400 (3 February 1812).

42. The price of 6 percent stock fell from an average of 103 in 1810 to 78½ by 1814, and 3 percent stock fell from 65⅜ to 51⅜ over the same period. See Sidney Homer, *A History of Interest Rates* (New Brunswick, 1963), p. 297.

43. Brown, "Stephen Girard's Bank," claims that between 1810 and 1812 Girard brought to the United States 550 shares of United States stock at par, 950 shares of BUS stock at about $400, $20,000 in silver, and $600,000 in merchandise, for a total of about $1,235,000.

44. In a letter to Alexander Baring, for example (SGC, III, 125, #407, 25 August 1815), Girard indicated that for his real estate in Philadelphia alone he paid "more than one hundreth part of the taxes which are yearly levied in said city. . . ."

45. Of a total 25,000 shares of BUS stock, 18,000 were owned abroad. Thus, Girard's holding represented about 14 percent of all American-held shares.

46. SGC, II, 51, #216 (1 April 1812). The bank was eventually chartered. See SGC, II, 51, #377 (June 1812).

47. Hammond, *Banks and Politics,* p. 266.

48. Girard was in New Castle, Delaware, making final arrangements for the arrival of the *Good Friends.*

49. Brown, "Stephen Girard's Bank," p. 34.

50. Ibid.

51. SGC, II, 51, #302 (5 May 1812).

52. Ibid., #298 (May 1812).

53. Ibid., #299 (5 May 1812). This warning no doubt referred to Girard's wife, the former Mary Lum, who went mad shortly after their marriage and was confined in the Pennsylvania Hospital.

54. Ibid., #304 (5 May 1812).

55. Ibid., #337 (20 May 1812). For Bollman's ideas on banking see H. E. Miller, *Banking Theories in the United States before 1860* (Cambridge, 1927).

56. SGC, II, 248 (20 May 1812).

57. SGC, II, 51, #336 (20 May 1812).

58. Recall that Ingersoll's letter of 5 May expressed concern that Girard and *some others* were about to open an unincorporated bank. Such an association would have been in violation of the law.

59. The effective rate of interest thus becomes approximately 6.38%.

60. Apparently the attempt here was to justify Girard's exceeding the 6 percent limit imposed on loans by the state's usury law.

61. SGC, III, 125, #479 (23 May 1812).

62. SGC, II, 248, (9 May 1812).

63. For tax purposes, in 1811 the Bank of the United States was valued at $75,000.00 and the implied valuation of Simpson's dwelling was $8,062.50. See SGC, II, 450.

64. SGC, II, 248 (6 June 1812).

65. Ibid. (June 1812).

66. Ibid.

67. For a complete record of the capital stock see: SGC, III, 94, #1, p. 99; #2, p. 98; #4, p. 112; #5, p. 112.

68. SGC, III, 94, #1, p. 80.

69. Ibid., p. 59.

70. Ibid., p. 140.

71. SGC, II, 393.

72. SGC, II, 53, "V" letters, #1764 (5 November 1813).

73. SGC, II, 125, #88 (5 November 1813).

74. See SGC, II, 249 (2 November 1813).

75. SGC, III, 125, #88 (5 November 1813).

76. SGC, II, 393-94.

77. SGC, III, 91, #241 (9 March 1813).

78. Ibid., #255 and #256 (18 March 1813).

79. SGC, II, 51, #328 (16 May 1812).

80. Ibid., #402 (10 June 1812).

81. SGC, III, 125, #497 (10 June 1812). The Orders in Council were rescinded on 23 June but war had already been declared.

82. SGC, II, 51, #504 (28 August 1812).

83. Redlich, *Molding of American Banking,* p. 61.

84. SGC, II, 248 (9 July 1812).

Chapter 3

1. SGC, III, 147.

2. Nicholas Wainwright, *History of the Philadelphia National Bank* (Philadelphia, 1953), pp. 28–29.

3. *American State Papers,* Finance, 2:566–67, #375.

4. SGC, II, 248 (May 1812).

5. An attempt to outlaw unchartered banks had failed in the Pennsylvania legislature earlier that year but was sure to arise again in the next session.

6. SGC, II, 51, #464 (July 1812).

7. SGC, II, 51, #470 (27 July 1812).

8. SGC, III, 91, #25 (27 July 1812).

9. SGC, II, 51, #474 (3 August 1812).

10. SGC, II, 51, #480 (6 August 1812).

11. SGC, III, 91, #31 (7 August 1812).

12. Louis Hartz, *Economic Policy and Democratic Thought, Pennsylvania, 1776–1860* (Cambridge, 1948), pp. 47–48.

13. Leighton P. Stradly, *Early Financial and Economic History of Pennsylvania* (New York, 1942), p. 65.

14. William M. Gouge, *A Short History of Paper Money and Banking in the United States* (1833) (New York, 1968), p. 56.

15. Hammond, *Banks and Politics,* p. 184.

16. Ibid., p. 185.

17. Raymond Walters, Jr., *Alexander James Dallas, Lawyer-Politician-Financier* (New York, 1969), p. 173.

18. SGC, III, 91, #183 (15 January 1813).

19. SGC, II, 248 (22 January 1813).

20. SGC, II, 248 (26 January 1813).

21. SGC, II, 248 (11 February 1813).

22. SGC, II, 52, #99 (5 March 1813).

23. The bill to tax unincorporated banks also failed to pass.

24. Henry Adams, *The Writings of Albert Gallatin* (Philadelphia, 1879), 1:532–33.

25. SGC, II, 149.

26. *American State Papers,* Finance, 2:626, #393.

27. Parish Letter Books, Folio 216 (16 March 1813). These manuscripts

are in the possession of the New York Historical Society, New York City. Hereafter cited as PLB.

28. Brown, "Stephen Girard's Bank," p. 41.

29. SGC, II, 248 (26 March 1813, 31 March 1813), and SGC, II, 52, #126.

30. SGC, II, 248 (1 April 1813).

31. PLB, Folio 235 (2 April 1813).

32. *American State Papers,* Finance, 2:647, #399.

33. Robert Lone, *Federal Financing* (New York, 1931), p. 54.

34. SGC, III, 91, #300 (16 April 1813).

35. SGC, III, 91, #300, #357, #422, #481, #547, #618, #684, #740.

36. PLB, Folio 284 (27 April 1813).

37. SGC, II, 52, #208 (14 May 1813).

38. SGC, III, 125, #33 (25 May 1813).

39. SGC, III, 125, #34 (28 May 1813). Such a new loan would depress the market price by increasing the supply of government stock available. Those who anticipated a new issue would therefore postpone purchases.

40. SGC, II, 248 (27 May 1813).

41. SGC, II, 248 (28 May 1813).

42. SGC, III, 125, #36 (29 May 1813).

43. SGC, II, 52, #226 (30 May 1813).

44. Girard chose the Bank of America (New York), the State Bank at Charleston, the Planter's Bank of Savannah, and the Boston State Bank.

45. SGC, II, 248 (10 June 1813).

46. SGC, III, 94, #1, p. 78.

47. SGC, III, 125, #79 (25 October 1813).

48. SGC, III, 94, #1, p. 78.

49. SGC, III, 240 (24 October 1813).

50. SGC, III, 125, #79 (25 October 1813).

51. SGC, III, 125, #109 (27 December 1813).

52. SGC, II, 53, #426 (3 January 1814).

53. SGC, III, 125, #115 (5 January 1814).

54. SGC, II, 470 (13 April 1814).

55. SGC, II, 249 (December 1813).

56. SGC, II, 53, #15 (7 January 1814).

57. SGC, II, 53, #22 (13 January 1814).

58. Hartz, *Economic Policy and Democratic Thought,* pp. 66–67.

59. In the end, some forty-one banks with combined capitals of $17 million were authorized. With the passage of the bank bill on 21 March 1814, thirty-seven institutions began operations, four of which were in Philadelphia. See Gouge, *Paper Money and Banking,* p. 57 and Stradley, *Early Financial and Economic History of Pennsylvania,* p. 66.

60. SGC, III, 125, #122 (10 January 1814).

61. The essence of this argument can be traced in some form back to the

sixteenth- and seventeenth-century debates over the crown's right to grant monopolies, patents, charters, etc.

62. Recall that this was the basis for the legal opinion of Dallas and Ingersoll on the legality of Girard's bank in 1812.

63. The state of Pennsylvania owned a large share of the Bank of Pennsylvania and forced the Philadelphia Bank to pay a bonus of $135,000 for a charter. In addition, the state was allowed to subscribe to $300,000 worth of the latter's capital stock in return for a like value of U.S. 6 percent bonds, selling at less than par, with an option to buy an additional $400,000 in stock. The Farmer's and Mechanic's Bank of Philadelphia was chartered in 1809 with the state as "partner."

64. This reference is to the federal bank-note tax of 2 August 1813.

65. SGC, III, 91, #733 (12 November 1813).

66. SGC, II, 53, #25 (14 January 1814).

67. SGC, II, 53, #37 (19 January 1814). William J. Duane (1780–1865) was the son of William Duane, editor of the pro-Jeffersonian *Aurora*. The younger Duane was first elected to the state legislature in 1809 and later (1819) became chairman of the Committee on Banks. Duane became an intimate of Girard's, acted as his solicitor, and drafted his will, in which he was named executor.

68. SGC, II, 53, #48 (22 January 1814).

69. SGC, II, 53, #38 (19 January 1814).

70. SGC, II, 54, #90 (9 February 1814).

71. SGC, II, 249 (18 February 1814).

72. SGC, II, 54, #178 (21 March 1814).

73. SGC, III, 125, #265 (12 February 1815).

74. Brown, "Stephen Girard's Bank," p. 46.

Chapter 4

1. SGC, III, 147–50.

2. SGC, II, 393.

3. SGC, II, 250 (29 August 1814).

4. Wainwright, *Philadelphia National Bank,* p. 39.

5. SGC, II, 250 (4 October 1814).

6. SGC, II, 250 (6 October 1814).

7. Section V of the BUS charter limited the bank's sale of 6 percent stock and other bonds to $2 million per year and required fifteen days' notice thereof to the secretary of the treasury.

8. Brown, "Stephen Girard's Bank," p. 131.

9. SGC, II, 54, #404 (19 October 1814).

10. SGC, III, 125, #240 (24 October 1814).

11. SGC, II, 54, #473 (8 December 1814).

12. SGC, II, 54, #410 (24 October 1814).

13. SGC, II, 54, #411 (30 October 1814).

14. SGC, II, 54, #435 (11 November 1814).

15. SGC, II, 250 (12 November 1814).

16. SGC, III, 125, #250 (25 November 1814).

17. Ironically, the deciding vote against the bank was cast by the Speaker of the House, Langdon Cheves, who was to accede to the presidency of the bank in 1820.

18. SGC, II, 55, #67 (88 February 1815).

19. Hammond, *Banks and Politics,* p. 230.

20. SGC, II, 55, #100 (13 March 1815).

21. SGC, III, 94, #1, p. 84.

22. SGC, III, 125, #325 (4 June 1815).

23. SGC, III, 125, #331 (12 June 1815).

24. SGC, III, 125, #339 (18 June 1815).

25. SGC, III, 91, #1573 (1 July 1815).

26. SGC, III, 125, #475 (16 October 1815).

27. SGC, III, 147–50.

28. SGC, III, 125, #480 (18 October 1815).

29. Walters, *Alexander James Dallas,* p. 206.

30. Redlich, *Molding of American Banking,* pp. 250–51.

31. Clarke and Hall, *Legislative and Documentary History of the Bank of the United States* (New York, 1967), pp. 613–21. For purposes of subscription, 6 percent stock was valued at par, 7 percent stock at 106.51, and 3 percent stock at 65.

32. Redlich, *Molding of American Banking,* p. 251.

33. SGC, III, 126, #176 (11 May 1816).

34. SGC, II, 58 (8 April 1816).

35. SGC, II, 58 (10 April 1816).

36. SGC, II, 58 (15 April 1816).

37. Clarke and Hall, *History of the Bank of the United States,* p. 622.

38. Ibid., p. 762.

39. Brown, "Stephen Girard's Bank," p. 134.

40. SGC, III, 126, #263 (17 August 1816).

41. The other government-appointed directors were John Jacob Astor of New York and A. Buchanon of Baltimore.

42. SGC, II, 60 (27 August 1816).

43. Brown, "Stephen Girard's Bank," p. 137.

44. SGC, III, 94, #1, p. 147.

45. SGC, III, 126, #117 (29 March 1817).

46. Ibid.

47. SGC, III, 126, #246 (5 August 1816).

48. SGC, III, 126, #279 (6 September 1816).

49. Redlich, *Molding of American Banking,* p. 254.

50. Dallas died three months later (16 January 1817) without seeing the BUS in full operation or the resumption of specie payments.

51. *American State Papers,* Finance, 4:283, #672.

52. SGC, II, 393.

53. SGC, III, 126, #425 (31 December 1816).
54. *American State Papers,* Finance, 4, #705, #2 (1 February 1817).
55. Ibid.
56. Hammond, *Banks and Politics,* pp. 247–48.
57. SGC, III, 126, #39 (28 January 1817).
58. *American State Papers,* Finance, 4:502–3, #705.
59. SGC, III, 126, #67 (13 February 1817).
60. SGC, III, 126, #78 (26 February 1817).
61. SGC, III, 126, #80 (28 February 1817).
62. SGC, III, 126, #112 (19 March 1817).
63. SGC, III, 126, #79 (27 February 1817).
64. SGC, III, 126, #90 (5 March 1817).
65. SGC, III, 126, #93 (8 March 1817).
66. SGC, III, 126, #336 (29 October 1816).
67. SGC, III, 126, #378 (29 November 1816).
68. SGC, III, 126, #413 (15 December 1816).
69. SGC, III, 126, #7 (7 January 1817).
70. SGC, II, 65 (31 December 1817).
71. Ralph C. H. Catterall, *The Second Bank of the United States* (Chicago, 1903), pp. 51–52.
72. SGC, III, 126, #291 (7 October 1818).
73. SGC, III, 126, #320 (1 November 1818).
74. Clarke and Hall, *History of the Bank of the United States,* p. 714.
75. SGC, III, 126, #404 (7 January 1819).
76. SGC, III, 126, #412 (12 January 1819).
77. SGC, III, 126, #417 (21 January 1819).
78. SGC, III, 126, #418 (22 January 1819).
79. SGC, III, 126, #427 (31 January 1819).
80. SGC, II, 393–94; and SGC, III, 94, #2, p. 100; #3, p. 126.

Chapter 5

1. Anna J. Schwartz, "The Beginning of Competitive Banking in Philadelphia, 1782–1809," *Journal of Political Economy* 55(1947):417.
2. Wainwright, *Philadelphia National Bank,* pp. 10–13.
3. Ibid., p. 15; and Holdsworth, *Financing an Empire,* p. 162.
4. Redlich, *Molding of American Banking,* p. 245.
5. Schwartz, "Competitive Banking," p. 431.
6. Redlich, *Molding of American Banking,* p. 39.
7. Schwartz, "Competitive Banking," p. 431.
8. Redlich, *Molding of American Banking,* pp. 38, 19.
9. SGC, II, 41, #313 (10 May 1812).
10. SGC, III, 125, #480 (23 May 1812).
11. SGC, II, 41, #387 (6 June 1812).
12. SGC, III, 91, #1 (2 June 1812).

13. SGC, III, 91, #3 (4 June 1812).

14. SGC, II, 248 (5 September 1812).

15. SGC, III, 91, #1 (2 June 1812).

16. SGC, III, 91, #48 (7 September 1812).

17. SGC, III, 91, #97 (27 October 1812).

18. SGC, II, 248 (27 October 1812).

19. SGC, III, 91, #5 (8 June 1812).

20. SGC, II, 248 (10 June 1812).

21. SGC, III, 91, #6 (12 June 1812).

22. SGC, III, 91, #20 (15 July 1812).

23. The Farmer's Bank of Lancaster was concerned about the acceptability of its notes since, like Girard's bank, it was an unchartered operation. Founded as a limited partnership in June 1810, its applications for a charter in 1810 and 1811 were refused. Eventually the Farmer's Bank was chartered under the terms of the Pennsylvania Banking Act of March 1814.

24. SGC, III, 94–95.

25. Some early exceptions were the Bank of America, the Farmer's Bank of Lancaster, and the Bank of Delaware.

26. SGC, III, 91, #1539 (17 May 1815).

27. SGC, II, 248 (11 September 1812).

28. SGC, II, 248 (5 October 1812).

29. SGC, II, 248 (26 October 1812).

30. SGC, II, 250 (24 March 1814).

31. Van Fenstermaker, *American Commercial Banking,* p. 41.

32. SGC, II, 249 (21 January 1814).

33. SGC, II, 249 (8 February 1814).

34. SGC, II, 249 (12 February 1814).

35. SGC, III, 91, #893 (22 January 1814).

36. SGC, III, #147–50.

37. SGC, III, 91, #894 (22 January 1814).

38. SGC, III, 91, #928 (11 February 1814).

39. SGC, III, 91, #933 (16 February 1814).

40. SGC, III, 91, #969 (9 February 1814) and #1101 (5 February 1814), and elsewhere.

41. SGC, III, 91, #1185 (8 July 1814).

42. SGC, II, 250 (5 July 1814).

43. SGC, III, 91, #1282 (1 September 1814).

44. SGC, II, 250 (7 September 1814).

45. See table 7.

46. SGC, III, 91, #1378 (29 October 1814).

47. SGC, III, 91, #1400 (23 November 1814).

48. SGC, III, 91, #1417 (3 December 1814).

49. SGC, II, 55, #67 (18 February 1815).

50. SGC, II, 55, #100 (13 March 1815).

51. By an act of 3 March 1815, Treasury notes were to be exchanged for some $18,452,000 in 6 percent stock.

52. SGC, II, 55, #196 (18 April 1815).
53. SGC, II, 55, #199 (20 April 1815).
54. SGC, III, 91, #126 (3 July 1816).
55. SGC, II, 252 (8 July 1816).
56. SGC, III, 91, #132 (9 July 1816).
57. SGC, III, 91, #136 (16 July 1816).
58. SGC, III, 94, #1.
59. SGC, II, 393.
60. SGC, III, 94–95.
61. George Simpson died in 1822.
62. SGC, III, 92 (3 November 1825).

Chapter 6

1. Wildes, *Lonely Midas,* p. 214.
2. SGC, III, 126, #114 (20 March 1817).
3. SGC, III, 94, #1, p. 99; #2, p. 98; #4, p. 112; #5, p. 112.
4. Although technically Girard's bank had no capital stock in the equity sense, the bank's books utilized this terminology.
5. For example, the Philadelphia Bank's charter limited liability to the amount of the "joint stock" of the company, and the Farmer's and Mechanic's Bank charter set maximum liabilities at twice the capital stock. See Holdsworth, *Financing an Empire,* 1:156 and 196.
6. A classic example of such a flow of specie was the eastward movement of gold and silver immediately preceding the suspension of specie payments in 1814.
7. By 1798, the Bank of England had come to accept as a norm the ratio of one to three, which reappeared as the "Palmer Rule" in 1832 and which dominated the market as late as 1914. See J. Keith Horsefield, "The Cash Ratio in English Banks before 1800," *Journal of Political Economy* 57 (1949):74.
8. Simpson, *Biography of Stephen Girard,* pp. 146–47.
9. SGC, III, 94, #2, p. 94 and p. 110.
10. SGC, III, 92 (16 June 1827).
11. SGC, III, 95, #4, pp. 102–7, 116.
12. SGC, III, 92 (10 December 1827).
13. SGC, III, 92 (15 December 1827).
14. SGC, II, 54, #438 (13 November 1814).
15. SGC, II, 54, #416 (15 November 1814).
16. SGC, II, 54, #416 (19 November 1814).
17. SGC, II, 54, #461 (5 December 1814).
18. Brown, "Stephen Girard's Bank," p. 51.
19. SGC, II, 55, #164 (7 April 1815).
20. SGC, II, 55, #172 (10 April 1815).
21. SGC, II, 55, 187 (13 April 1815).

22. SGC, II, 393, 394.

23. SGC, II, 393–94.

24. SGC, III, 91, #199 (4 February 1813).

25. SGC, III, 92 (17 January and 17 April 1824).

26. SGC, III, 126, #114 (20 March 1817).

27. SGC, II, 248 (30 October 1812).

28. SGC, III, 92 (21 July 1823).

29. SGC, III, 91 (30 November 1816).

30. SGC, III, 92 (1 March 1824).

31. SGC, III, 92 (2 May 1826).

32. SGC, III, 91, #150 (12 August 1816).

33. Simpson, *Biography of Stephen Girard,* p. 117.

34. SGC, III, 92 (24 October 1824).

35. SGC, III, 91, #177 (4 January 1813).

36. SGC, III, 91, #1612 (26 August 1815).

37. SGC, III, 92 (21 July 1823).

38. SGC, III, 92 (29 January 1824).

39. SGC, III, 92 (17 April 1824).

40. SGC, III, 92 (12 March 1828).

41. SGC, III, 93 (18 September 1829 and 27 September 1831).

42. SGC, II, 249 (21 January 1814).

43. SGC, II, 393.

44. Simpson, *Biography of Stephen Girard,* p. 115.

45. Redlich, *Molding of American Banking,* p. 63.

46. Simpson, *Biography of Stephen Girard,* p. 115.

47. Ibid.

48. See certificate #123 on David Parish's list. SGC, II, 52, #126.

49. SGC, II, 248 (9 April 1813).

50. SGC, II, 248 (9 April 1813).

51. SGC, II, 248 (15 April 1813).

52. SGC, III, 93 (1 August 1829).

53. SGC, III, 93 (27 February 1830).

54. This was possible because notes discounted actually yielded 6.38 percent to the bank. Since interest was deducted at the date of discount, the borrower paid $6 for the use of $94 rather than $100. At Girard's bank, this rate was typically rounded to 6.4 percent.

55. SGC, III, 93 (6 February 1829).

56. SGC, III, 92 (23 May 1827).

57. Simpson, *Biography of Stephen Girard,* pp. 114–15.

58. SGC, III, 125, #122 (10 January 1814). Apparently Girard chose to forget his arrangement of the preceding November with the trustees of the Bank of the United States wherein he agreed to pay 3 percent interest on the funds they deposited, or he considered it a special case.

59. SGC, II, 393.

60. SGC, III, 59 (7 September 1814).

61. SGC, III, 126, #94 (9 March 1817).

62. SGC, III, 125, #122 (10 January 1814).

Chapter 7

1. Simpson, *Biography of Stephen Girard,* p. 165.
2. SGC, III, 93 (31 December 1829).
3. SGC, III, 94, #2, p. 110; #4, p. 116.
4. SGC, III, 91, #1454 (18 January 1815).
5. SGC, III, 91, #1460 (23 January 1815).
6. SGC, III, 91, #1476 (8 February 1815).
7. SGC, III, 91, #1477 (8 February 1815).
8. SGC, II, 393.
9. Paul Trescott, *Financing American Enterprise* (New York, 1963), p. 37.
10. Redlich, *Molding of American Banking,* p. 49.
11. Girard used this stock to help capitalize his bank in 1812. It was not until 1827 that the final dividend of 1.75 percent was paid on BUS stock.
12. The town of Girardville commemorates the banker's involvement in this area.
13. See Sidney Homer, *A History of Interest Rates* (New Brunswick, 1963), pp. 286–87 and 295–99.
14. Margaret Myers, *The New York Money Market* (New York, 1931), 1:46.
15. Redlich, *Molding of American Banking,* p. 10.
16. Myers, *New York Money Market,* 1:48.
17. Redlich, *Molding of American Banking,* p. 47.
18. SGC, III, 92 (29 January 1824).
19. SGC, III, 92 (12 March 1828).
20. SGC, III, 93 (27 September 1831).
21. SGC, III, 94, #2, pp. 73 and 94.
22. SGC, III, 94, #4, pp. 102–7.
23. Gras, *Massachusetts First National Bank of Boston,* p. 60.
24. SGC, III, 93 (6 February 1829).
25. Joseph Martin, *A Century of Finance* (New York, 1969), p. 97.
26. Anna J. Schwartz, "Gross Dividends and Interest Payments by Corporations at Selected Dates in the Nineteenth Century," National Bureau of Economic Research, Trends in the American Economy in the Nineteenth Century, Studies in Income and Wealth, vol. 24 (Princeton, 1960), pp. 431–32, 442, 436.

Chapter 8

1. SGC, III, 93 (27 December 1831).
2. Ibid. (30 December 1831).

3. Ibid. (30 December 1831).
4. SGC, II, 470 (9 January 1832).
5. SGC, III, 93 (10 January 1832).
6. SGC, II, 470 (13 January 1832).
7. SGC, III, 93 (14 January 1832).
8. Ibid. (16 January 1832).
9. SGC, II, 470 (30 January 1832).
10. Ibid. (1 February 1832).
11. Ibid. (20 February 1832).
12. SGC, III, 93 (5 March 1832).
13. Ibid. (22 February 1832).
14. SGC, II, 470 (14 April 1832).
15. SGC, III, 93 (16 April 1832).
16. Ibid. (26 April 1832).
17. SGC, II, 470 (January 1832).
18. SGC, III, 95, #5, p. 285.
19. Ibid., p. 112.
20. Ibid., p. 117.
21. Ibid., p. 295.
22. SGC, II, 470 (8 June 1832).
23. SGC, III, 93 (9 June 1832).
24. Ibid. (24 July 1832).
25. Ibid. (1 August 1832).
26. Ibid (27 December 1832).
27. Ibid (27 December 1832).

Note on Manuscript Sources

The basic manuscript sources utilized in the writing of this book are from the Stephen Girard Collection. The original documents are held by Girard College in Philadelphia with access by permission only. The collection has been microfilmed and is available in this form at the American Philosophical Society Library in Philadelphia.

The collection is divided into three series. Series I is a catalogue of incoming and outgoing correspondence and contains 14 reels of microfilm. Series II consists of 482 reels of microfilm, dealing with a variety of subject matter such as shipping papers, general mercantile papers, and accounts of Stephen Girard's Bank. Series III covers much the same subject matter as Series II and contains 167 reels of film. Listed below are the major sources for the present study.

Series II, Reels 51–60

Letters received, 1812–1816. This is general correspondence dealing with all facets of Girard's commercial and financial transactions, as well as personal correspondence.

Series II, Reels 248–252

Incoming bank correspondence. These letters deal only with the operation of Stephen Girard's Bank and for the most part are the records of daily transactions between the cashiers of other institutions and Girard's cashiers, George Simpson (1812–1822) and Joseph Roberts (1822–1831).

156

Series II, Reel 470

Bank letters. This is a collection of more general correspondence dealing with Stephen Girard's Bank. Most letters are from or to Stephen Girard and span the years 1812–1835.

Series II, Reels 393–94

Bank Balance Sheets. These reels contain the quarterly balance sheets of Stephen Girard's Bank. As such they constitute the most basic source of quantitative evidence concerning the bank.

Series III, Reels 91–93

Bank letters. This group contains the basic outgoing correspondence of the bank. Again, most of the letters are routine and deal with day-to-day operations.

Series III, Reels 1–37

Bank records. These reels contain such specialized information as listings of notes discounted and the daily record books of the tellers at Stephen Girard's Bank.

Series III, Reels 125–26

Letters sent. This is a collection of outgoing letters on a variety of subjects, including banking. It covers the years 1812–1819.

Series III, Reels 147–50

Cash books. These reels record the bank's holdings of gold, silver, and bank notes between 1812 and 1833.

Series III, Reels 94–95

Bank ledger books. These reels contain the general ledgers of Stephen Girard's Bank between 1812 and 1832. This material supplements the data available in the quarterly balance sheets.

Index

Treasury of United States (*cont.*)
 loan of 1813, 32
 notes, 116
 relations with Stephen Girard's
  Bank, 61, 66 f.
 resumption, 58, 83 f.
 southern funds, 50
 Stephen Girard's Bank as
  depository, 50 f.
Trenton Banking Company, 74
Trustees of Bank of the United States
 relations with Stephen Girard's
  Bank, 21

 sale of Bank of the United States,
  18 f.
 stock of the Bank of the United
  States, 14

unchartered banks
 decline, 5
 early importance, 5
 European, 90 f.
 growth of, 28
 laws against, 5, 28, 37 ff.
Union Bank of Maryland, 136

Willing, Thomas, 3 f.